The Importance of
South Carolina
in the
American Revolution

The Importance of
South Carolina
in the
American Revolution

Aliene Shields Humphries

Charleston, SC
www.PalmettoPublishing.com

The Importance of South Carolina in the American Revolution

First Edition

Paperback ISBN: 978-1-63837-391-9
Hardcover ISBN: 978-1-63837-392-6
eBook ISBN: 978-1-63837-393-3

Dedication

This book is dedicated to Daniel Gilbert, my fifth great-grandfather. He was born in 1731 and died in 1805. Lt. Gilbert served in the French and Indian War and the American Revolution. He moved his family to South Carolina in 1786, and our family has been here ever since. Daniel Gilbert is buried in Spartanburg county, South Carolina.

Thank you, Daniel Gilbert. May your memory live on.

Table of Contents

Acknowledgements

I want to thank all of my family and friends for their belief in me and encouragement. The book is possible because of the untold hours contributed by Brittney Evans; she is a friend, contributor, and editor. Jack Parker and his book have been a wonderful resource. Tony Scotti has contributed through friendship and writing. John McCabe wrote an excellent piece to help us appreciate what treasure is right here in South Carolina. Thank you to everyone who has driven me down the highways and backroads to find many of these "hidden treasures" in our great state. Oh, what all the victories and losses our ancestors endured! But they persevered; and with their help, South Carolina helped the 13 colonies become the United States of America.

Introduction

By John Franklin McCabe of Columbia, South Carolina

The term "Genius Loci" originated in Roman Mythology referring to the protecting spirits guarding historical places. In modern times, the term refers to the "spirit of the place" and its distinctive atmosphere.

Standing on the plains of Gettysburg Battlefield or on the shores of Normandy, one usually is overcome with a feeling of awe owing to the intense history of the events that occurred in these august places. During the American Revolution, locations like Lexington and Concord, Massachusetts, Saratoga, New York, and Yorktown, Virginia stand out as locations where valiant Patriots fought and died for Independence from Great Britain. Yet no other colony had more military engagements than South Carolina during the conflict, making the entire state Genius Loci.

From 1775–1783, The Revolution in the South, a civil war by any definition pitting neighbor against neighbor and families against each other, with allegiances changing sides with the winds of war, saw over 400 skirmishes, clashes, and epic battles all over the colony. While visiting Charleston and seeing the harbor where the British Navy's Invasion Forces were repelled by an ingenious and dedicated South Carolina regimental forces at Fort Sullivan (now Fort Moultrie), or touring the fortifications of the Star Fort at Ninety-Six, or climbing up King's Mountain, history enthusiasts of all ages will most certainly experience the awe-inspiring feeling of place, the Genius Loci.

While driving through Ox Swamp in Clarendon County, one can imagine Lt. Colonel Banastre Tarleton gasping in frustration, "...as for this damned old fox, the devil himself could not catch him", giving a name to the legend Colonel Francis Marion, the Swamp Fox. One can take a stroll down Front Street in Georgetown and see the tall ships' masts lining the wharves while British Regulars occupy the town fearing the siege from Marion which was certainly inevitable.

The Southern Campaign of the American Revolution was the British strategy to roll up the southern colonies after the Continental Army and the Northern Theater were stymied near Monmouth, New Jersey, beginning in 1779 with the siege of Savannah. What began well for the British did not end well as Lord Cornwallis was forced to surrender to General George Washington at Yorktown in 1781. What happened in between Savannah and Yorktown earned South Carolina the moniker "The Battleground of the Revolution."

After capturing Savannah, the British turned their sights on Charleston, the richest city in the Thirteen Colonies. Even though the Continentals put up a valiant, defense, Charleston under

Gen. Benjamin Lincoln fell to the British in May of 1780, leaving patriot militias led by such men as Marion, Thomas Sumter the Gamecock, and Andrew Pickens the Wizard Owl to keep the cause alive. These partisan bands harassed and raided forts, outposts, and caravans of the British Army and were effectively the only resistance fighting force left for the Americans. Their objective during this period was to weaken the British Army and buy time until the arrival of General Nathanael Greene and the Continental Army from the north.

Curious tourists can see where General Daniel Morgan outwitted Lt. Col. Tarleton at the Cowpens Battlefield in Cherokee County near the town of Cowpens and sense the importance of this patriot victory and the military prowess of Gen. Morgan and his brilliant use of militias, continentals, and dragoons in concert.

These same tourists can travel just a short way up the road to feel the power of Kings Mountain Battlefield where patriot militias defeated Major Patrick Ferguson and his loyalist militias, proving that militias can be a formidable fighting force in their own right.

History enthusiasts will not be light on opportunities to continue exploring Revolutionary Sites in South Carolina. Travel to destinations like The Cheraws, The Waxhaws, The Congarees, and Musgrove Mill to stand in the same place where brave soldiers risked and sometimes gave their lives for the cause of Liberty. Move on south to Jacksonboro where the first assembly met waiting for the British to evacuate Charleston. See where Captain John Laurens lost his life at The Battle of Combahee River a full year after Yorktown, and after he had served Gen. Washington as his aide de camp before heading back to South Carolina to drive the British out of the colony.

*M*ove on up to Round O and see the vast countryside and dense woods where General Nathanael Greene bivouacked his Southern Army waiting to triumphantly march into Charleston following the British surrender.

Drive on up to the center of South Carolina to Columbia, the Capital City created when Colonel Thomas Taylor who fought at Quinby Bridge under Gen. Sumter sold four square miles of his own plantation to establish a centrally located state capital. This is most important to me because I am writing this piece while standing at the convergence of these four square miles that my fifth great grandfather Thomas Taylor helped establish Columbia. Yes, every day of walking through the Capital City, viewing the beauty of the Statehouse, the beautiful gardens of the Governor's Mansion, the historic homes and the streets named for so many revolutionary heroes fills me with the spirit of the Genius Loci.

I reference all of these locations in South Carolina, but there are many more. Aliene Humphries' *The Importance of South Carolina in the American Revolution* is most certainly a fabulous deep dive into multiple sites around the state. We are certainly fortunate as South Carolinians, as well as

Americans, for true Modern Day Patriots like Aliene Humphries who has compiled and published this fabulous book for every student of history and all American Patriots now and in the future.

Without the bravery and tenacity of the soldiers and citizens of South Carolina, the British Southern Strategy may have succeeded. Fortunately, the Patriot Cause was strengthened and the British Army was weakened in South Carolina which resulted in the victory at Yorktown.

Enjoy this guide to the rich Revolutionary War history here in South Carolina.

Dum Spiro Spero
While I Breathe I Hope

Foreword

Growing up in the 1940s and 50s in Delaware, I knew of the Battle of Brandywine, the wintering at Valley Forge, a few battles in New York, New Jersey and Boston. What I did not know until about 2000, was that South Carolina was a leader in the fight for freedom from British rule.

I discovered that on October 26, 1765, 150 volunteers from Charleston, SC threatened to burn the Tax Stamps held in Fort Johnson. The result was that the *HMS Speedwell* removed all the stamps and sailed out of the Charleston harbor. This action is all but forgotten because it is prior to the Revolution's accepted starting date, but is very significant since it relates to the stamp problems in New England, AKA the Boston Tea Party, on December 16, 1773, a full 8 years later.

Two days after the Battle of Lexington, April 19, *1775*, word of the action at Lexington, Massachusetts had not yet reached South Carolina on April 21, 1775. This is when the Americans in Charleston broke into the British Magazines at Cochran's, Hobcaw, and the State House Armory, stealing all the weapons and ammunition for the American cause.

The Rutledge brothers, the Pinckneys, Christopher Gadsden, the Horrys, and Charles Alston, met to drink and discuss politics at McCrady's Tavern, When DeLancey came to Charleston, SC, in 1771, he was probably arguing over politics, liberty and separation from England with these local Charlestonians. Patriot, Dr. John Haley, killed Peter DeLancey, a prominent New York Tory, in a duel at a Charleston tavern on August 15, 1771, again well before the Battle of Lexington, Peter DeLancey was the son of New York Royal Lt. Gov. James DeLancey. The Delanceys were a prominent Manhattan, NY, family. The killing of Peter DeLancey revealed the Patriot sentiments of the south and in 1776 resulted, in part, with Loyalist Brig. Gen. Oliver DeLancey raising and commanding a provincial regiment (three battalions), known as DeLancey's Brigade, consisting of light horse troops, to fight the Patriots. The Patriots referred to this Brigade as "DeLancey's Cowboys", as they drove cattle to Manhattan to supply the regular British regiments stationed there.

Before the Battle of Eutaw Springs, SC on September 8, 1781 the British troops involved in that battle were to reinforce Gen. Cornwallis at Yorktown, Virginia. However, due to the exhausting fight at Eutaw Springs, some of the British retired to the Old White Meeting House, the forerunner to the White Presbyterian Church, to rest and recover instead. The other troops retreated to another location, but did not go to Yorktown. Note: Only an Episcopal Church, owned by the King of England, was called a Church then, the other denominations were called Meeting Houses.

South Carolina was instrumental in the Revolutionary War with over 500 violent encounters between the British, Patriots and Loyalists throughout the state. For some Loyalists, the war was an opportunity to rob their neighbors and become wealthy, as was the case of the Harrison brothers. Two brothers, Robert and Samuel, were killed during the war, but Col. John Harrison survived the war to retire in East Florida, a British safe haven for Loyalists, as a wealthy man.

These actions put South Carolina in the forefront of the American Revolutionary War, even though the residents of the northern states are almost totally unaware of South Carolina's early and direct contribution to the American Revolution. South Carolina contributed much to the Revolutionary War's final outcome with the removal of British loyalists from the state and the defeat of Lord Cornwallis at Yorktown, Virginia leading to the winning of American independence. In fact, the Revolutionary War in South Carolina was our country's first Civil War with many fighting against relatives and neighbors.

The Importance of South Carolina in the American Revolution brings attention to the little known Revolutionary War sites in South Carolina, so that the history and beauty of South Carolina can be experienced first hand. While traveling to the various sites, keep in mind that there were few bridges or roads during the late 1700s. The roads that did exist were dirt and usually only wide enough for one wagon. Travel was by foot, horse, wagon or buggy. Clean drinking water was another problem as it was practically non-existent, necessitating adding about one half rum to a glass of water to kill the deadly germs in the water, particularly on ships. There were no vaccines to fight Smallpox and other diseases. leading to many deaths on both sides of the conflict. All in all, it was a dangerous time to be alive.

John (Jack) Parker
Parker's Guide to the Revolutionary War in South Carolina
parkerdist@shtc.net

Preface

It is quite difficult to determine when a historical event begins. The American Revolution (spirit) began years before the actual American Revolutionary War. John Adams, our first vice president and second president, summed it up best, "The Revolution was effected before the war commenced. The Revolution was in the minds and hearts of the people; a change in their religious sentiments of their duties and obligations. This radical change in the principles, opinions, sentiments, and affections of the people, was the real American Revolution."

There were many contributing factors that helped lead up to the shots fired at Lexington and Concord, Massachusetts on April 19, 1775. (Please look at the chronological Timeline of Events for events and dates, and note the importance of the French and Indian War. No historical event occurs in a vacuum.) 1775–1783 were very tumultuous years for the 13 colonies/states. Thank goodness for France's help beginning in 1778. It became very rebellious in South Carolina especially after the Fall of Charleston in 1780—a true civil war of brother against brother and neighbor against neighbor, every single family member was affected. Please note, Blacks' and Indigenous peoples' roles in the Revolutionary War weren't as simple as many today would like to reduce it to. I have left these groups out of the book and they will be discussed in detail in another book, along with religious beliefs and groups.

Hopefully you will travel our great state of South Carolina with its diverse terrain, to learn of the critical importance of the Southern Campaign in our fight for independence. There were tremendous challenges of geography, primitive one-lane dirt roads, few bridges, poor maps, diseases, lack of food, temperature extremes, wild animals, and more adversities to overcome than just fighting.

Please note, many sites are on private lands—No Trespassing! Just because locations or GPS coordinates are given, permission is _not_ given to trespass. South Carolina sites are often held by private homeowners. Thankfully, the Daughters of the American Revolution, the highway historic markers program, the National Register of Historic Places, and others have placed many markers at key places/sites. Please respect the rights and efforts of private landowners and DO NOT TRESPASS.

Please note the author is aware of some inconsistencies, inaccuracies, misinformation, etc. in this book. please remember many of these events took place over 250 years ago and information and "popular legend" have been handed down. One example of this is regarding Francis Marion—he was referred to as a "fox" for his elusive tactics, but not as the "Swamp Fox." There is no evidence of the "Swamp Fox" being used until 1800. This book is my attempt to bring awareness and increase interest during the 18th century in our great state. Please excuse any inaccuracies and inconsistencies.

There were over 250 battles and skirmishes fought in South Carolina throughout the Revolutionary War. We are so fortunate that these lands remain in "protective hands," or in their natural state; they aren't strip malls, "concrete jungles" on top of hallowed ground, but most of these sites are not developed and are waiting for us to "discover" them. Hopefully this book and others will help you learn about our first veterans and enjoy these sites. And help give a better understanding of the Liberty Trail, American Battlefield Trust, South Carolina Battleground Trust, and individuals who are helping to make more historical sites available and preserve history. Enjoy your ride through history and see what brave families endured to make this a free and independent country for themselves and all of us. By saving the land where our nation was created, and by telling these stories, we are honoring the sacrifice of the patriots who fought and died for our freedom. Many of the patriots who are laid to rest on the hallowed grounds that you will visit are creating a priceless legacy for all future generations. Enjoy the ride through history and learn *The Importance of South Carolina in the American Revolution.*

Map of South Carolina

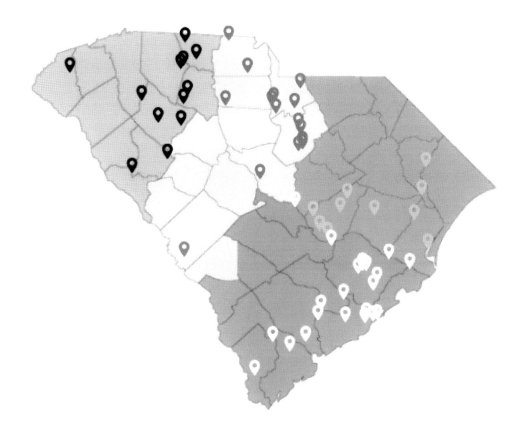

Glossary

1. <u>Abatis:</u> a defensive obstacle formed by felled trees with sharpened branches facing the enemy
2. <u>Ammunition:</u> bullets, cannon balls, and gunpowder, and any other objects that can be fired
3. <u>Articles of Confederation:</u> an agreement between the thirteen colonies to form a single government under the United States of America. It served as the country's first constitution. Its drafting by a committee appointed by the Second Continental Congress began on July 12, 1776, and an approved version was sent to the states for ratification on November 15, 1777. The Articles of Confederation came into force March 1, 1781, after being ratified by all 13 states.
4. <u>Backcountry:</u> Any land settled 50 miles inland from the coast.
5. <u>Badge of Merit:</u> General Washington established the "Badge of Merit" later referred to as the Purple Heart. It was originally awarded for singular meritorious action.
6. <u>Boycott:</u> a refusal as part of an organized group to buy from, or deal with a store, company, person, or nation
7. <u>Bayonet:</u> a blade attached to the end of a musket
8. <u>Cash crop:</u> a crop that is grown to be sold rather than use by the farmer
9. <u>Colony:</u> an area of land that is under control of a country, but not fully part of the country
10. <u>Conspire:</u> to plan together secretly to do something
11. <u>Constitution:</u> a set of documents and laws that define the government of a country
12. <u>Continental Congress:</u> a group of delegates from each colony or state. It became the first governing body of the United States of America.
13. <u>Continental Army:</u> the official army of the United States that was established by the Continental Congress
14. <u>Cooper:</u> a barrel maker
15. <u>Declaration of Independence:</u> the document that announced the American colonies now considered themselves independent and they would no longer answer to the authority of Great Britain
16. <u>Democracy:</u> a type of government that is ruled directly by the people
17. <u>Dragoons:</u> dragoons were originally a class of mounted infantry, who used horses for mobility, but dismounted to fight on foot. From the early 17th century onward dragoons were trained for combat with swords and firearms from horseback.
18. <u>Enlisted:</u> to sign up for; to agree to serve
19. <u>Epidemic:</u> an infectious disease that spreads quickly through a community or group

20. <u>Federalist:</u> a person who supported the adoption of the Constitution
21. <u>Garrison:</u> a military force that is set up to defend a fort or city
22. <u>Gill:</u> is a unit of measurement in the 18th Century used for liquids and is equal to about a half a cup, or 4 fluid ounces
23. <u>Guerilla Warfare:</u> a type of military action using small groups of fighters to carry out surprise attacks against enemy forces
24. <u>Hessians:</u> soldiers from the German land of Hesse who came to fight for the British
25. <u>Heroism:</u> the act of a woman showing bravery
26. <u>Hero:</u> the act of a man showing bravery
27. <u>High Hills of Santee:</u> is a long, narrow hilly region in the western part of Sumter County, South Carolina.
28. <u>Howitzer:</u> a Revolutionary War variant of the cannon, whose barrels were much shorter in length but much larger in diameter than the cannon. Howitzers averaged around eight and 13 inches in diameter and around three feet in length. The typical effective range of these weapons was around 750 yards. These chambered guns also fired explosive powder-filled shells with a timed fuse that was lit by the firing charge, and were much more maneuverable during battle thanks to their shorter barrel length.
29. <u>Indigo:</u> a tropical plant grown in South Carolina, which was formerly cultivated for its violet blue dye. It was one of the state's cash crops.
30. <u>Legislature:</u> a branch of government that has the power to make laws
31. <u>Linen:</u> cloth made from flax
32. <u>Litter:</u> a carrying device for wounded or dead soldiers
33. <u>Loyalist:</u> a person in America who stayed loyal to Britain and the king
34. <u>Malaria:</u> is a mosquito-borne infectious disease that can affect humans and animals.
35. <u>Militia:</u> citizens who were prepared to fight. They held drills a few times a year and provided their own weapons and gear.
36. <u>Minutemen:</u> part of the Massachusetts militia that was prepared to fight at a moment's notice
37. <u>Moat:</u> a deep, wide ditch surrounding a fort, typically filled with water and intended as a defense against attack.
38. <u>Monarchy:</u> a government where the power and laws are made by a single person called a monarch
39. <u>Musket:</u> a smooth bore gun with a long barrel that fired lead balls
    note: A musket has a smooth bore like a shotgun. When it is loaded with "buck and ball", it has one regular musket ball and two or three buckshot loaded into it so that they will all become projectiles with one firing of the musket. This is a very deadly combination against charging troops.

40. <u>Overmountain Men</u>: were American frontiersmen west of the Appalachian Mountains, who fought in the American Revolution.

41. <u>Parliament</u>: the main governing body of the Britain

42. <u>Patriot</u>: an American that wanted independence from Britain

43. <u>Pension</u>: a sum of money given to people after they retire from service or profession

44. <u>Plantation</u>: several fields that are under cultivation, usually by enslaved people

45. <u>Proprietor</u>: a person given ownership of a colony

46. <u>Rice</u>: another South Carolina's cash crops during the Colonial Era

47. <u>Ratify</u>: to formally approve a document

48. <u>Rations</u>: a fixed portion of food allotted to a soldier or person when supplies are low

49. <u>Repeal</u>: to officially cancel something, such as a law

50. <u>Redcoat</u>: a nickname for the British soldiers taken from their bright red uniforms. They were also called lobsterbacks.

51. <u>Redoubt</u>: a temporary or supplementary fortification

52. <u>Republic</u>: a type of democratic government where people elect officials to represent them

53. <u>Revolution</u>: the overthrow of a government to establish a new system

54. <u>Rout</u>: a disorderly retreat of defeated troops.

55. <u>Royal colony</u>: a colony controlled by a monarch

56. <u>Sedition</u>: conduct or speech inciting people to rebel against the authority of the state

57. <u>Smallpox</u>: a disease that spreads easily from person to person, causing chills, fever, and pimples that scar, can also cause death

58. <u>Sons of Liberty</u>: a group of patriots organized by Samuel Adams to protest the Stamp Act and other actions of the British government

59. <u>Sortie</u>: an attack made by troops coming out from a position of defense

60. <u>Spy</u>: a person who covertly obtains secret information from the enemy

61. <u>Stamp Act</u>: a tax placed on the American colonies by the British government. It taxed all sorts of paper documents including newspapers, magazines, and legal documents.

62. <u>Tory</u>: political party that believed that the king should keep firm control of the colonies

63. <u>Tobacco Hogsheads</u>: hogshead is a large barrel used to store and/or transport packed, or "prized" leaf tobacco. (Usually 48" long and 30" in diameter and weighed about 1,000 pounds)

64. <u>Treason</u>: the crime of betraying one's country, especially by attempting to kill the sovereign or overthrow the government.

65. <u>Treaty of Paris 1783</u>: a treaty signed by both the United States and Britain that ended the Revolutionary War

66. <u>Volley</u>: when a large number of muskets fire at once

67. <u>Whigs:</u> American political party that mostly believed the colonies should be allowed to govern themselves

68. <u>Yellow Fever:</u> an illness that can cause high fever, chills, nausea, and kidney and liver failure; liver failure causes the skin to become yellow, giving the disease its name.

Military Organization

Army Organization and Battle Tactics

Britain's military was the best trained and most well disciplined military in the world at the time of the American Revolution, thus most countries' military organizations followed the same basic pattern. It should be noted that depending upon the number of men in fighting condition the size of a brigade, division, and army could vary greatly at any given time.

Regiments were the primary fighting force of the Revolutionary War. At the time of the unit's formation a British regiment consisted of exactly 811 men. It was led by a Colonel, and staffed by 40 junior officers, 72 non-commissioned officers, 24 drummers, 2 fifers, and fielded by 672 privates. The American regiments averaged around 470 men fit for service at time of formation. Each regiment was broken into 1 or 2 battalions, which were then broken down into 10 companies, eight of which were regular "center" companies, while the remaining two were "flank" companies. Companies were comprised of 40 privates, 3 corporals, 1 ensign (2nd Lieutenant), 1st Lieutenant, and a Captain. The "flank" companies would often function independently throughout the course of a battle.

Normal battle tactics during a battle entailed that the two armies march toward one another, shoulder to shoulder, and usually in ranks of about three men deep. When the opposing sides were within range, orders were given to halt, present arms, to fire, and then to reload. After several volleys, one side would gain the upper hand and would begin to close the distance towards the enemy. This typically culminated in a full out charge at close quarters; sabers, bayonets, and rifle butts were used to sweep the enemy from the field and claim victory.

It should be noted that while the two armies were marching towards each other, field artillery was being used to thin out the battle lines and confuse unseasoned soldiers on the battlefield. The most common types of field artillery used were 3, 6, and 18-pounder guns, named for the weight of shot that the guns fired. Larger cannons and mortars were often used in sieges given their destructive capabilities, they lobbed large-caliber projectiles in high arcs onto their targets. Howitzers, with shorter barrels and larger calibers compared to cannons, were also utilized by both sides.

During the French and Indian War colonists worked and fought with indigenous warriors, learning their unique battle tactics that worked in the dense forests of America, which were no longer present in Europe. The American colonists took what they had learned during the French and Indian War and used what is known as guerilla warfare to fight the British. The main fighting force behind the guerrilla warfare was the non standardized militia. Militia generally refers to the army or other fighting force that is composed of non-professional fighters, citizens of a country, who may perform military service during a time of need. They attacked supply lines and ambushed British troops moving between battlefields and camps. It was these skirmishes off of the battlefield that wore down the British and led to Cornwallis' surrender at Yorktown, Va.

Military Rations and Uniforms

	American Forces	**British Forces**
Uniform	Navy blue coats with white breeches*	Red coat with bleached white breeches**
Rations	-1 ½ pounds of flour or bread -1 pound of beef or fish OR ¾ pounds of pork -1 gill of whiskey	-1 ½ Pounds flour or Bread -1 pound of beef or a ½ pound of pork -¼ pint of canned Peas or 1 ounce of rice -1 ounce of butter -1 ½ gills of Rum

*Prior to the military force being standardized, the army wore a hodgepodge of colors, mainly brown.
**British Dragoons wore green coats instead of the standard red.

Though both armies were supposed to receive regular rations, due to weather, road conditions, the season, and other supply chain issues, rations could at times be hard to get for the fighting soldiers of both armies. That is why strategically occupied towns in South Carolina's backcountry, like Ninety Six and Camden, were so important to both the British and the Americans.

Military Officer Ranks

Military ranking during the American Revolutionary War (1775–1783) can be confusing at times as changes have been made to officer rankings over the past 200 plus years. Though the American army did initially follow the British ranking system, they soon developed their own which changed a few times during the war. It is important to note that the rank of Brigadier General both in the past and today is only ever used during a time of war and a Brigadier General can hold several ranks at one time. If there are several ranks listed on one line, that means that they are of equal rank and pay, but go by different names depending on which branch of the military they are a part of.

American Forces	British Forces
General (Gen.)	General (Gen.)
Lieutenant General (Lt. Gen.)	Lieutenant General (Lt. Gen.)
Major General (Maj. Gen.)	Major General (Maj. Gen.)
Brigadier General (Brig. Gen.)	Brigadier General (Brig. Gen.)
Colonel (Col.)	Colonel (Col.)
Lieutenant Colonel (Lt. Col.)	Lieutenant Colonel (Lt. Col.)
Major (Maj.)	Major (Maj.)
Captain (Capt.)	Captain (Capt.)—Captain-Lieutenant (Capt. Lt.)
Subaltern (Sub.)	Lieutenant (Lt.)—1st Lieutenant
Lieutenant (Lt.)	Ensign (Ens.)—2nd Lieutenant—Cornet
Ensign (Ens.)	
Sergeant Major (Ser. Maj.)	
Sergeant (Ser.)	
Corporal (Cor.)	
Private (Pvt.)	

Other Branches of the Military

It takes many moving parts and different actions to win a war, an army alone does not decide the victor. Navies played a key role in keeping either side bottled up and stopping supplies from making it to ports. The British navy, just like the army, was the best in the world. By the end of the American Revolution Britain had 478 ships at its disposal, while America boasted 31 vessels. Despite the lack of ships within the American navy, they also contracted privateers to help harass the British navy and supply ships coming to and from England throughout the war. Privateers helped America win the war by capturing over 300 British vessels.

Both armies also used what were known as Legions, which were a mix of infantry and cavalry. Cavalry units were quick and small. Used mainly to scout, hit and run raids, to support the main army during battle, cavalry were trained in multiple weapons and how to fight both on foot and from atop a horse. Legions quickly gained fame and notoriety, especially in the South as they could move quickly through the Backcountry and were quite versatile. British Lt. Col. Banastre Tarleton and American Lt. Col. Henry "Light Horse Harry" Lee were both commanders of top performing Legions throughout the American Revolution.

No military is complete without the use of spies, and both the British and the American military employed numerous spies from all backgrounds to help gain the upperhand throughout the war. Men, women, and even children carried secret encoded messages across battle lines, hoping their small sacrifice would help turn the tide of war in their preferred sides' favor.

Chronological Order of Events

While the colonies were still under British rule in the 1740s through the 1750s, a great migration occurred in what was deemed the backcountry using the Great Wagon Road. The backcountry was defined as any land at least 50 miles inland. The Great Wagon Road ran from Pennsylvania all the way down to Savannah, Georgia. Most of the immigrants that settled into the backcountry territory were of Scots-Irish descent, with a few English and German settlers as well. Tensions rose between the new settlers and the indigenious population they were pushing out of this "newly discovered" land. It is from these tensions and the lack of concern and help that Charleston gave the backcountry that vigilantes arose to "protect" and regulate society through law and order in the backcountry; they called themselves, Regulators. The Regulators did what they said they would, but would also see fit to "discipline" any whom they deemed being of a "lower sort" than themselves, sowing the seeds of internal conflict that would later play out bitterly during the American Revolution in the backcountry.

1754 saw the American colonies enter into a larger global conflict that had lasting effects for all the major empires of the 18th century. After years of small skirmishes about land disputes between French and English colonists, the French and Indian war began in earnest in May of 1754. While the British Empire was ultimately successful in fighting off the French and claimed vast amounts of new fertile territory for their American colonists, it was a costly war that put the Empire in a bad financial position. The Treaty of Paris in 1763 might have ended the French and Indian War, but it showed the beginning of a revolutionary spirit and fervor that had begun to develop under the British's policy of salutary neglect towards their American colonies. And when the colonies rose up against the British, the bitter French seized the opportunity to once again fight the British by aiding the patriots in their fight for freedom.

Listed are the events and dates that either took place in South Carolina or tremendously affected our state.

Date: Event:

| February-10-1763 | **England, London:** The Treaty of Paris ends the Seven Years War, (French and Indian.) Left in debt from the war, Great Britain looked to the colonies for revenue. |

October-7-1763   **England, London:** Proclamation of 1763 banned settlement west of the Appalachian Mountains.

January-1-1764   **England, London:** The Currency Act prohibited the Colonies from printing their own money. First protest of the "Taxation without representation."

April-5-1764   **England, London:** Sugar Act imposed stricter trade regulations and duties on sugar and molasses. It is the first law aimed at raising money for the Crown.

March-22-1765   **England, London:** The British imposed the Stamp Act on printed matter such as legal documents and newspapers, the first direct tax on the colonists.

March-24-1765   **England, London:** Parliament passed the Quartering Act requiring the colonies to provide barracks and supplies for British troops.

November-1765   <u>SC:</u> Stamp act goes into effect in South Carolina.

March-18-1766   **England, London:** After having the colonists refuse to import British goods for a year, the British Parliament (under pressure from British merchants) repealed the Stamp Act.

                 The Declaratory Act affirms Parliament's right to make laws binding the American colonies.

June-29-1767   **England, London:** The Townshend Revenue Acts created new import duties for the colonists.

March-5-1770   **MA, Boston:** King's troops fired and killed five civilians in an attack soon to be known as the Boston Massacre. Among the killed includes Crispus Attucks, a free black. All Townshend duties were removed except the tax on tea before the British backed off and troops left Boston.

May-10-1773   **England, London:** English Parliament passed the Tea Tax.

December-3-1773 <u>**SC, Charleston:**</u> First Charleston Tea Party

December-16-1773 **MA, Boston:** A group of patriots led by Sam Adams, and dressed as Mohawk Indiens dumped 342 chests of tea overboard in protest of taxes at the "Boston Tea Party." The cost was estimated at more than $1,700,000 in today's money.

January-20-1774 **England:** News of Boston Tea Party shocked London.

May-20-1774 **MA, Boston:** The Coercive Act closed the port of Boston, bringing the Massachusetts government under Crown control, it allowed the British troops to be quartered on private property, and allowed those accused of crimes while administering British policy to be tried outside Massachusetts.

September-5-1774 **PA, Philadelphia:** First Continental Congress met to organize a resistance to British tyranny, responded to the Coercive Acts by adopting a policy of nonimportation of English goods and drew up a list of grievances for King George III.

March-23-1775 **VA, Richmond:** At the Second Virginia Convention Patrick Henry made his famous "give me liberty or give me death" speech.

March-30-1775 **England, London:** King George III, required New England to trade exclusively with England, endorsed the New England Restraining Act.

April-18-1775 **MA, Boston:** Famous midnight ride of Paul Revere warning "the British were coming," also riding that night were William Dawes and Dr. Samuel Prescott.

April-19-1775 **MA, Concord:** Dr. Samuel Prescott reached Concord with the message that the British were coming; which allowed the militia time to destroy supplies and prepared to fight.

MA, Lexington: Battle of Lexington. Lieutenant Colonel Francis Smith with a force of 1,800 men had one wounded in action at Lexington. The

American forces, led by Captain John Parker with 70 militia men, had 8 killed and 10 wounded in action. The American forces originally had 170 men, but after a long wait were told to disburse and wait to be called. Lexington and Concord were known as "the shot heard around the world." Conclusion: a British victory.

MA, Concord: The battles occurred when the British went to Concord to confiscate arms and ammunition. American forces were commanded by Colonel James Barrett who had 3,703 men; 49 were killed in action, 39 wounded in action and 5 captured. The British forces were commanded by Major John Pitman with 1,800 men; 3 killed and 4 wounded in action. The British started to retreat to Boston keeping the militia at bay with occasional cannon fire by the reinforced British troops. The British would not leave Boston again until they evacuated a year later.

New England: Post rider Israel Bissell began his ride through the Colonies to deliver the news of Lexington.

SC, Charleston: Patriots seized the arriving British mail.

April-21-1775   **SC, Charleston:** Patriots seized all gunpowder supplies from the public magazine.

May-10-1775   **PA, Philadelphia:** Second Continental Congress convened.

May-20-1775   **PA, Philadelphia:** The 13 colonies agreed on the articles of union and confederation.

May-22-1775   **SC, Charleston:** Henry Laurens wrote the events at Lexington and created in South Carolina "an amazing readiness to contribute to the common cause."

May-26-1775   **PA, Philadelphia:** Congress declared a new name: "The United Colonies of America."

June-2-1775   <u>SC:</u> The Provincial Congress of South Carolina asserted solidarity with the colonies.

June-9-1775   <u>SC:</u> The Provincial Congress of South Carolina prohibits exports of rice and corn and began stockpiling supplies.

June-10-1775   **Continental Congress:** John Adams proposed the creation of the Continental Army.

June-15-1775   **PA, Philadelphia:** The Congress unanimously voted to appoint George Washington General and Commander-in-Chief of the new Continental Army.

June-16-1775   **Continental Congress:** Congress appointed generals in the Continental Army and created supporting military services.

June-17-1775   **MA, Breed's Hill:** The first major fight between British and American troops occurs. At the Battle of Bunker Hill (Breed's Hill) the British succeeded in taking the hill, but lost half their force. British forces were commanded by General William Howe who had 3,000 men; 269 killed in action, 826 wounded in action. The American forces were commanded by General Israel Putman, they suffered 400 to 600 casualties in retreat. Massachusetts lost 115 killed in action, 305 wounded in action and 30 captured at this battle. The siege of Boston lasted from 17 May 1775 until 17 March 1776. William Prescott is credited as saying, "don't fire until you see the whites of their eyes."

July-5-1775   **Continental Congress:** Congress issued a petition declaring its loyalty to the king, George III, and stating its hope that he would help arrange a reconciliation and prevent further hostilities against the colonies. Four months later, King George III rejected the petition and declared the colonies in rebellion.

July-12-1775   <u>SC, Fort Charlotte:</u> A Continental force of 51 men led by Major James Mayson captured Fort Charlotte without firing a shot. The Fort was commanded by Captain George Whitfield, had only 15 men and his family. The rangers managed to capture 1,000 pound of gunpowder, 18 cannons and much musket and cannon balls.

July-17-1775 *SC, Ninety Six:* Captain Moses Kirkland who commanded the fort at Ninety Six decided to change sides to Loyalist. He invited Colonel Fletchall of the Loyalist Militia to take the fort. Fletchall sent 300 men and took the fort.

July-27-1775 **SC:** Henry Laurens, President of the Council of Safety of South Carolina, urged Captain Clement Lempriere to purchase gunpowder, lead, and muskets for the colony, but to rely on force only as a last resort.

August-15-1775 **SC:** Lord William Campbell, Governor of South Carolina appealed to the House of Assembly for aid, admitting that "the power of Government were wrested out of my hands, I can neither protect, nor punish, therefore with the advice of council, I apply to you and desire that in this dreadful emergency you will aid me in enforcing the law."

August-28-1775 **SC:** Apparently unaware of Loyalist sympathies in the interior of the colony, a native of Charlestown, South Carolina observed, "Everything here is suspended, but warlike preparations."

September-5-1775 **SC, Charleston:** The Council of Safety adopted a more proactive program for the defense of the province, calling on the militia to stand "in readiness in time of alarm."

September-14-1775 **SC:** Rebels captured strategically important Fort Johnson on James Island.

November-19-1775 *SC, Ninety Six:* A truce ended two days of fighting between Loyalists and Patriots at the fortified settlement of Ninety Six. The Loyalists had 1,800 men, while the fort was manned by 600 Continentals under Major Andrew Williamson. Conclusion: a draw.

November-25-1775 **SC:** The South Carolina Congress resolved that "the colony is in a state of actual alarm" and sent additional militia into the interior to reinforce those fighting against the Loyalists.

December-22-1775   ***SC, Cane Break:*** A Patriot force commanded by Colonels Richard Richardson, William Thompson, Thomas Polk and Alex Martin had a combined force of 4,000 men. British Loyalists were under William Cunningham. The Patriot force was to break up a gathering of loyalists in South Carolina. The Americans attacked and the Loyalist resistance quickly collapsed.

Continental Congress: Congress named Esek Hopkins commodore of the fledgling American navy. Soon after, Congress authorized privateering, and issued rules for dealing with enemy vessels and plunder.

February-19-1776   **SC, Charleston:** The Provincial Convention, apprehensive of a British attack, voted to summon militia to defend the city.

March-3-1776   **SC, Yamacraw:** The Battle of the Rice Boats took place in the Savannah River on the border of Georgia and South Carolina. The Battle pitted the American militia against the Royal Navy. After British warships attacked a group of merchant ships carrying rice, Georgia militia and South Carolina Whigs set *HMS Inverness* on fire along with *HMS Nelly* and 3 other ships.

March-14-1776   **SC, Sandy Point:** The Battle of Sandy Point. South Carolina naval tenders sailing up the river encountered a Loyalist ship coming down the river with a cargo of flour. The Loyalists ran the ship aground and the tenders were unable to free it. When the tide came in the tenders freed it and sailed it into Charleston.

March-26-1776   **SC, Charleston:** The Provincial Congress of South Carolina approved a new constitution and government for the province. The legislature is now the General Assembly of South Carolina; the group elected John Rutledge as president, Henry Laurens as vice president, and Secretary John Huger are elected to govern the newly independent state.

March-28-1776   **SC:** South Carolina declared independence from Great Britain.

April-2-1776   **SC:** The General Assembly empowered its new president, John Rutledge to design and have made a Great Seal of South Carolina.

May-2-1776   <u>**France and Spain:**</u> Both countries agree to supply arms to the patriots in the British colonies.

May-29-1776   <u>**SC, Charleston:**</u> A sloop from St. Eustatius arrived in Charlestown, South Carolina, with 10,000 pounds of powder. The master of the vessel stated that the French West Indies ports were now open to the Americans and French warships were protecting the rebel vessels.

May-30-1776   <u>**SC:**</u> British General Sir Henry Clinton agreed to undertake an effort to capture the city of Charlestown.

June-3-1776   <u>**SC, Sullivan's Island**</u>: Colonel William Moultrie informed President Rutledge that a British landing was imminent, and vowed to "make the best defense I can with what I have."

June-8-1776   <u>**SC:**</u> Colonel Moultrie received notice that General Sir Henry Clinton had landed troops on the southern tip of Long Island,(Isle of Palms). Moultrie in turn ordered American troops to occupy the northern part of Sullivan's Island. The British were not able to come across the inlet.

June-23-1776   <u>***SC, Charleston:***</u> Commodore Peter Parker notified General Sir Henry Clinton that he would land on the mainland tomorrow on the flood tide if the wind was from the south. Parker and his fleet were thwarted by a sandbar for nearly three weeks.

June-25-1776   <u>***SC:***</u> Off the coast of South Carolina, after spending three weeks getting his fleet across a sandbar, Commodore Peter Parker's postponed plans to bombard the fort on Sullivan's Island due to unfavorable wind and tidal conditions.

June-27-1776   <u>***SC:***</u> Off the coast of South Carolina, Commodore Peter Parker gives the signal to get underway towards Sullivan's Island, but is again halted when the wind suddenly shifts to the opposite quarter.

June-28-1776 *SC, Charleston:* At about 10 AM Commodore Peter Parker's squadron opened fire on Fort Sullivan. To the surprise of the British, the fort's palmetto log wall absorbs the British shot like a sponge, preventing typical splinter injuries to the garrison. More surprising is the accurate and effective fire directed by Colonel Moultrie at the British fleet. Their two largest warships *HMS Bristol* and *HMS Thunder* suffered extensive damage and severe crew losses. Commodore Parker suffers painful physical injuries and the embarrassing loss of his breeches. *HMS Sphinx* lost her bowsprit. The *Actaeon* and *Syren* ran aground, smaller frigates were damaged. Moultrie's attack cost Parker 261 injured and dead. American casualties were slight. This is the battle where Sergeant William Jasper rallied the troops by rising the South Carolina flag.

SC, Sullivan's Island: At the Battle of Fort Sullivan Island, American forces commanded by Colonel William Moultrie had a force of 436 men, 17 killed and 20 wounded in action. British forces were under command of General Sir Henry Clinton, who had a force of 9 ships; he had 64 killed and 131 wounded in action. Conclusion: an American victory.

June-29-1776 *SC:* Inspired by his stunning success in repulsing Commodore Peter Parker's naval squadron, William Logan sent a gift of a hogshead of old Antigua rum to Colonel Moultrie.

July-2-1776 **Continental Congress:** Congress formally adopted Lee's resolution, asserting that the "United Colonies were, and of right ought to be, free and independent States, that all political connection between them and the state of Great Britain is and ought to be, totally dissolved." The vote would have been unanimous except New York abstained.

July-3-1776 **PA, Philadelphia:** During the same day, Congress considered Jefferson's "Declaration for Independence," and decided to continue their examination at the next session.

July-4-1776 **PA, Philadelphia:** After much debate and compromise the Second Continental Congress adopted the Declaration of Independence. As President of the proceedings John Hancock is the sole signer and remarked that "We must all hang together." Benjamin Franklin replied, "Or we will most assuredly hang separately." "THE BIRTH OF A NATION"

July-8-1776 **PA, Philadelphia:** The Liberty Bell in center Philadelphia rang in order to gather citizens of the city for the reading of the "Declaration of Independence."

July-15-1776 ***SC, Lyndley's Fort:*** July 14th, a group of Patriot settlers had taken refuge in Lyndley's Fort. That evening, Capt. Jonathan Downs of the Little River District Regiment of Militia and 150 men sought refuge with the settlers. At 1:00 a.m. in the morning of the 15th, 88 indigenous people and 102 Loyalists painted as indigenious persons, led by Capt. David Fanning of the Upper Saluda Loyalist Militia, attacked Lyndley's Fort, not knowing beforehand that Capt. Downs and his men were there. The Loyalists departed at 4:00 a.m. after learning that Major Williamson's forces were on their way, leaving several dead including two of their chief warriors. As they left, the Patriots captured thirteen and sent the prisoners to the jail at Ninety Six.

July-22-1776 **PA, Philadelphia:** Congress, sitting as a committee of the whole, considered the printed draft of John Dickinson's "Articles of Confederation." They would be adopted in November 1777.

July-30-1776 **Continental Congress:** Debate on the "Articles of Confederation" continued. On the subject of voting in Congress, Dr. Franklin believed that for the smaller colonies to have an equal vote, they should have to give equal money and men. John Witherspoon (NJ), however, feared that, "smaller states will be oppressed by the great ones."

August-2-1776 **SC, Charleston:** News of the Declaration of Independence arrived today.

August-12-1776 ***SC, Little River:*** Major Andrew Pickens, with a detachment of 25 men, were attacked by a group of 135 Cherokee Indians while on a reconnaissance mission. The American troops killed several Indians who then broke off the fight and withdrew. The battle was also known as the "Ring Fight."

September-3-1776   **PA: Philadelphia:** President John Hancock writes to the Assemblies of North and South Carolina and Georgia, urging the return of delegates to Congress. The matters before the Congress were "of the utmost importance to the welfare of America" and the States should be fully represented.

September-9-1776   **Continental Congress:** Congress adopts the name "United States of America" on this day. Resolved, that in all continental commissions, and other instruments, where heretofore, the words United Colonies have been used, the style be altered for the future to the "United States."

September-16-1776   **PA, Philadelphia**: Congress voted to raise without delay, 88 battalions to serve for the duration of the war. Each state received a quota ranging from 15 battalions each from Massachusetts and Virginia to one each from Georgia and Delawwere. To spur enlistment, soldiers would be offered bounties, which included $20 and 100 acres of land.

September-17-1776   **France, Paris:** Silas Deane promised Robert Morris that he would forward to America vast quantities of military stores in October, including clothing for 20,000 troops.

September-20-1776   **PA, Philadelphia:** Congress adopted a new body of Articles of War, which was formulated to resolve the problems of discipline, administration, organization, recruitment, etc., which had persistently plagued General Washington.

September-21-1776   **SC, Charleston:** Patriot General Robert Howe on his way north from Georgia warned the authorities of the state that the islands off their coast were undefendable and urged every effort be made to remove the livestock to prevent seizure by the British. Stripping the islands of livestock and all other property would have been a most effective deterrent to enemy occupation.

September-24-1776   **PA, Philadelphia:** Congress prepared instructions for the guidance of those agents who would be appointed to negotiate a treaty with France.

October-1-1776   **PA, Philadelphia:** Benjamin Franklin and Robert Morris received information that the French were going to purchase arms and ammunition in Holland and send them to the West Indies for the Americans.

October-18-1776   <u>SC:</u> The South Carolina Assembly approved the revision on this day of the Constitution adopted in March 1776.

October-22-1776   **PA, Philadelphia:** Congress elected Arthur Lee of London as Commissioner to France, "Mr. Jefferson having informed Congress that the state of his family will not permit him to accept the honor of going as their Commissioner to France." Benjamin Franklin was the second Commissioner chosen.

October-26-1776   **PA, Philadelphia:** Benjamin Franklin accompanied by his grandsons, Temple Franklin, age 17, and Benjamin Franklin Bache, age 7, departed from Philadelphia for France. The *Reprisal* carried a cargo of indigo to pay the expenses of the mission of Benjamin Franklin, Arthur Lee, and Silas Deane.

November-19-1776   **PA, Philadelphia:** Congress sent a reminder "to several States, how indispensable it is to the common safety, that they pursue the most immediate and vigorous measures to furnish their quotas of troops for the new army, as the time of service which the present Army was enlisted in, is so near expiring."

November-29-1776   **PA, Philadelphia:** The Congress continued to approve support for the Northern Army. This day the members ordered medicines for scurvy, continued the hospital for contagious diseases at Fort George, and ordered that there be a garden near the general hospital for growing fresh vegetables.

January-1-1777   **PA:** George Washington authorized inoculation of the entire army against smallpox.

September-17-1777   **PA, Philadelphia:** Congress prepared to leave Philadelphia as the British approached and granted General Washington dictatorial powers with full responsibility for conducting war.

November-16-1777 **Continental Congress:** Richard Henry Lee's proposal for independence in June 1776 included a plan for all the colonies to form a union. After a year of debates, Congress passed the Articles of Confederation with hope of unifying the colonies into states.

November-17-1777 **Continental Congress:** Congress submitted the Articles of Confederation to the states for ratification.

November-23-1777 **France, Paris:** News of the British occupation of Philadelphia reached France. At a dinner party in France, a comment was made about General William Howe taking Philadelphia, to which Benjamin Franklin replied, "It is not Howe who occupies Philadelphia, but Philadelphia who occupies Howe."

March-21-1778 **PA, Valley Forge:** Brigadier General Frederick Von Steuben, frustrated with views of American troops, said, "in Europe when you tell a soldier to do a drill he does it without question. When you tell an American he asks "why" then does it better than anyone."

July-9-1778 **PA, Philadelphia:** Continental Congress approved the Articles of Confederation.

July-11-1778 **PA, Philadelphia:** The term "United States of America" first officially used.

September-14-1778 **PA, Philadelphia:** Congress elects Benjamin Franklin minister to France.

February-1-1779 **SC, Port Royal Island:** South Carolina militiamen prevented British forces from landing on Port Royal Island. The British under Captain Patrick Murray were ordered ashore to burn plantations. After militiamen sniped at the British force they withdrew. The brig HMS Lorge George Germaine bombarded houses.

February-3-1779 ***SC, Buford:*** American forces under the command of General William Moultrie had a force of 320 men, with 8 killed and 22 wounded in action; met the British led by Major Gardiner with 200 men. The British force was repulsed with heavy losses at the battle on Port Royal Island.

April-29-1779   *SC, Purrysburg:* A battle occurred when British Light Infantry troops and two battalions of the 71st Scottish Highlander Regiment, commanded by Lieutenant Colonel John Maitland, crossed the Savannah River from Abercorn, Georgia and invaded the colonial town of Purrysburg.

May-3-1779   *SC, Coosawahatchie River:* Patriot Lieutenant Colonel John Laurens with a detachment of light infantry went on a mission to rescue a rear guard. The British under Lieutenant Colonel John Maitland with 800 men and long range artillery kept the South Carolina infantry at bay. Laurens was wounded, placing Captain Richard Shubrick in charge, the detachment withdrew.

June-20-1779   *SC:* Battle of Stono Ferry. The American force had 1,200 men, with 146 killed or wounded, and 155 captured. The British had 900 men, with 26 killed and 163 wounded in action. Conclusion: Battle of Stono Ferry is another British victory.

August-14-1779   **PA, Philadelphia:** The Continental Congress approved a peace proposal that called for not only independence, but also the evacuation of North America by the British and free navigation of the Mississippi River.

September-27-1779   **Continental Congress:** John Jay is appointed minister to Spain, however, there is no hope of obtaining Spain's recognition of the fledgling republic. All Jay is able to accomplish is a loan of $170,000 to keep the Spanish covertly supplying the nation with war material.

March-29-1780   *SC, Charleston:* The Siege of Charleston lasted from March 29 until May 12. General Sir Henry Clinton arrived off the coast of Charleston with 90 troop ships and 14 ships of the line, with more than 8,500 soldiers and 5,000 sailors. American forces were commanded by Major General Benjamin Lincoln with 5,000 men, with 92 killed in action, 48 wounded in action, and 4,650 captured. British forces had 14,000 men, with 76 killed in action, 189 wounded in action and 70 captured. Conclusion: British victory.

April-14-1780   *SC, Monck Corner:* Battle of Monck Corner. The American force was commanded by General Isaac Huger with 500 men; 20 killed or wounded and 67 captured. British force led by Lieutenant Colonel Banastre Tarleton with 650 men; 3 wounded in action. Tarleton captured wagons of supplies and excellent cavalry horses. The battle cuts off communications between Lincoln and Charleston. Conclusion: British victory.

SC, Fair Lawn: The British converted Fair Lawn Plantation, also known as Fair Lawn Barony or Colleton Mansion, into a hospital and supply storeroom. Peter Colleton, the owner of the property, was a British loyalist and descendent of John Colleton, one of the original Lord Proprietors of the Carolina Colony. Fort Fair Lawn was built on the edge of the plantation's property. Its key location, at the head of the Cooper River and along both a coastal and inward road, rendered its defense strategically important.

May-6-1780   *SC, Lenud's Ferry:* The Battle of Lenud's Ferry was a small battle by some Continentals who escaped Moncks Corner. The American forces were led by Lieutenant Colonel William Washington and Colonel Abraham Buford with 350 men; 41 killed in action and 67 captured. British forces were commanded by Lieutenant Colonel Banastre Tarleton with 150 men, who had caught the Continentals by complete surprise.

May-12-1780   *SC:* Charleston surrendered on May 12. In a massive and humiliating defeat to the Patriots, General Benjamin Lincon and 5,400 American troops surrender to General Sir Henry Clinton. The British called this "Reverse Saratoga." British guns pounded the city for 42 days.

May-24-1780   *SC:* Lieutenant Colonel Banastre Tarleton while in pursuit of Governor Rutledge of South Carolina arrived at the plantation of Thomas Sumter. Sumter had fled to an American encampment at Salisbury, North Carolina. After searching and looting they set all the buildings on fire.

May-29-1780   *SC, Waxhaw:* Lieutenant Colonel Banastre Tarleton with cavalry destroyed a Virginia regiment under the white flag of surrender. Americans cut down by sword. This was known as Tarleton Quarters. American forces led by

Colonel Abraham Buford with 400 men; 113 killed in action, 203 wounded or captured. British forces had 270 men; 5 killed and 15 wounded in action. Conclusion: British victory. This became a battle cry as the Americans exploited the massacre.

June-3-1780   **SC, Camden:** General Charles Cornwallis traveled to Camden without trouble from local Patriot forces. This was mainly due to the heavy brutality of Lieutenant Colonel Banastre Tarleton.

June-6-1780   ***SC, Alexander's Old Field:*** Captain John McClure led a group of Patriots and surrounded a group of 200 Loyalists. They fired and began yelling at the Loyalists, forcing them to flee the area. This is the first American victory after the fall of Charleston.

SC, Camden: The British army takes over the town of Camden, a strategic supply spot on several main roads and waterways. General Cornwallis set up command at the Kershaw House.

July-1-1780   ***SC, Georgetown:*** Vice-Admiral Mariot Arbuthnot with Capt. John Plumer Ardesoif seized ships in Georgetown harbor and sent sailors upriver in armed barges to plunder Patriot plantations, effectively capturing the town for the British.

July-12-1780   ***SC:*** Battle of Williamson's Plantation (Huck's Defeat), Captain Christain Huck, a prominent Loyalist, led a mixed force of British dragoons and Loyalists from Rocky Mount. At Williamson's Plantation the Patriots launched a surprise attack inflicting complete defeat on the British forces. American forces led by Colonels William Hill, Edward Neal, Thomas Lacey and Winn with 250 men; 1 killed in action. British forces numbered 115 men; 86 killed or wounded and 29 captured. Those killed included Captain Huck. Conclusion: an American victory.

July-13-1780   ***SC, Cedar Spring:*** Colonel John Thomas was commanding a Spartan regiment of the South Carolina Patriot militia. He was warned that the Loyalist intended to attack his camp, when the attack began Loyalist ran into a planned ambush, they were beaten and quickly retreated.

SC, Gowen's Old Fort: Colonel John Jones was leading a force of Georgia Patriot militia when they surrounded and attacked a Loyalist camp. The Loyalists who were pursuing Colonel John Thomas's militia force were forced to surrender without any serious resistance.

July-16-1780   **SC, Earl's Ford:** British Major James Dunlap attacked a rebel camp under cover of darkness along the Pacolet River in South Carolina. The Loyalists stabbed many, even as they asked for quarter. The British withdrew before a decisive victory was achieved and a Patriot retaliatory raiding party was sent out.

July-30-1780   ***SC:*** Capture of Thicketty Fort (Anderson). Patriot forces numbered 600, led by Colonel Isaac Shelby, took the Loyalist held fort, located 10 miles from Cowpens, without firing a shot. This action preceded the Battle of Kings Mountain.

SC, Hanging Rock: Lieutenant Colonel William Davie and his North Carolina Patriot force ambushed 3 companies of Colonel Samuel Bryan's North Carolina Royalists. The ambush was in sight of a strong British post; most of the Loyalists were killed or wounded. After capturing all the weapons and horses the Patriots retired.

August-1-1780   ***SC, Rocky Mount:*** In the Battle of Rocky Mount, American forces are under Colonel Thomas Sumter, 600 men, with 200 killed or wounded. British forces are under Lieutenant Colonel George Trumbull with 300 men, with 14 killed, 29 captured.

August-8-1780   ***SC, Wofford's Iron Works:*** Captain James Dunlap with approximately 144 men was sent to capture Patriot supply wagons. They discovered the Patriot camp abandoned shortly after Colonel Elijah Clarke and his 600 man patrol left it. The Patriots set up an ambush for the Loyalists, the fight ended in hand-to-hand combat. The Loyalists were driven back. Both Dunlap and

Clarke were injured. The Patriots had 4 killed and 21 wounded in action. The Loyalists lost; 34 killed or wounded in action and 50 prisoners.

August-13-1780 <u>SC:</u> Major General Horatio Gates, in command of all American southern forces, pushed the men south to a point of exhaustion, in order to catch up with the British.

August-15-1780 <u>*SC, Cary's Fort:*</u> Colonel Thomas Sumter sent a detachment of his troops under the command of Col. Thomas Taylor to attack this Loyalist fort on the Wateree River being garrisoned by British regulars. The Patriot troops killed or captured the entire garrison along with all its supplies.

August-16-1780 <u>*SC, Camden:*</u> The battle of Camden was a major defeat for the Continental Army. General Horatio Gates overestimated the number of soldiers available for combat and was too late to withdraw when he realized his mistake. Major General Johann DeKalb was wounded and died later. The British captured much equipment. Gates rode away so hard and fast he left his army behind, and did not stop until he reached Hillsborough, North Carolina, 180 miles away. He was relieved of his command. American troops numbered 3,052 men; 900 killed in action, 150 wounded in action and 1,000 captured. British troops under General Charles Cornwallis had 2,239 troops, with 68 killed and 245 wounded in action.

August-18-1780 <u>*SC, Fishing Creek:*</u> Led by Lieutenant Colonel Banastre Tarleton, a force of 350 Loyalists located an American force led by General Thomas Sumter near Camden. Tarleton caught the Americans totally unprepared. This victory made Tarleton in the British eyes a national hero. He freed 100 British prisoners. American forces numbered 700 men, with 150 killed or wounded and 330 captured. British forces had 160 men, with 16 killed or wounded.

<u>*SC, Musgrove's Mill:*</u> This is another engagement that followed Camden and preceded Kings Mountain. Patriot Colonels Elijah Clarke and Isaac Shelby commanded a militia force that repelled an attack by Loyalists. The Americans made a stand at Musgrove's Mill, killing 63 Loyalists, wounding

90 and capturing another 70. American losses were 4 killed and 9 wounded. Conclusion: an American victory.

August-20-1780   <u>*SC, Great Savannah:*</u> After being promoted to Brigadier General, Francis (Swamp Fox) Marion was at Horse Creek Pass. He attacked the British, captured 22 prisoners and released 150 Maryland Continentals held by the British.

August-27-1780   <u>**SC, Kingstree:**</u> A large British force under Major James Wemyss was ordered to punish plantation owners for the concealment of arms and ammunition with the total destruction of the plantations. A smaller Patriot force led by Major John James was to determine the British strength. They hid in the brush, counted the British, skirmished, and killed, wounded or captured 30 British soldiers.

September-4-1780   <u>*SC, Blue Savannah:*</u> Following up with his success at Savannah, Francis Marion, the "Swamp Fox," and 52 of his men rode to the east to escape pursuing Loyalists. However another force of Loyalists over 250 strong came from the northeast. After routing the advance guard, Marion caused the main body to panic and flee. This broke the Loyalists in the area and attracted another 60 volunteers to the Patriot cause.

September-29-1780   <u>*SC, Black Mingo Creek:*</u> After discovering a British outpost, Colonel Francis Marion led a small group of Americans, approximately 50 men, he had 2 killed and 8 wounded in action. British forces numbered about the same but had 3 killed in action and 13 wounded or captured; they were led by Colonel John C Baal. Marion's force broke the Loyalists in a complete rout. This was a small skirmish which lasted only 15 minutes.

October-17-1780   <u>*SC, Kings Mountain:*</u> Major Patrick Ferguson's entire force of 1,100 Loyalists were either killed, captured or wounded in this engagement with Colonel William Campbell, leading 900 frontiersmen. The Loyalists depended on massed volleys and bayonets, while the Americans depended on the long rifle to pick off the Loyalists at long range. The Americans killed many Loyalists as they tried to surrender. The battle forced General Charles Cornwallis to abandon the invasion of North Carolina. American forces were also led by Colonels Cleveland, McDowell, Sevier and Shelby with 900 men; 28 killed in action and 62 wounded in action. British forces were commanded by Major Patrick Ferguson with 1,104 men; 225 killed, 163 wounded in action, and 716 captured.

October-25-1780   ***SC, Tearcoat Swamp:*** Colonel Francis Marion, at Britton's Neck, learned of Lieutenant Colonel Tynes' encampment at Tearcoat Swamp. He was able to call together 150 men and surprised the Loyalists. Lieutenant Colonel Tynes and his men were scattered, and a few days later Lieutenant Colonel Tynes and a few of his officers were captured by a detachment of Colonel Marion's commanded by Captain William Clay Snipes.

November-8-1780   ***SC, Ox Swamp:*** On the morning of November 8th, Lieutenant Colonel Banastre Tarleton learned that his enemy, Colonel Francis Marion was nearby, Lieutenant Colonel Tarleton and his British Legion quickly gave chase. Colonel Francis Marion, staying just ahead of the British Legion cavalry and fighting a series of delaying tactics with Major John James leading his rear guard, finally slipped away into the Ox Swamp. After a seven-hour chase, Lt. Col. Banastre Tarleton gave up the chase and swore "Come my boys! Let us go back and we will find the Gamecock. But as for this damned old fox, the devil himself could not catch him!"

November-9-1780   ***SC, Broad River:*** Fishdam Ford, South Carolina. British Major James Wemyss, commanded a force of 140 horsemen, attempted a surprise attack on General Thomas Sumter and his 300 man militia. Sumter managed to evade capture by Wemyss. Wemyss was the second most hated man in the British Army, and was wounded in the arm and knee. Casualties were light on both sides.

November-20-1780   ***SC:*** Battle of Blackstock's Plantation. American forces were under General Thomas Sumter with 1,000 men; 3 killed, 5 wounded in action. British forces were commanded by Banastre Tarleton who had 270 men; 50 killed or wounded.

December-4-1780   *SC, Rugeley's Mills:* A force of Continental dragoons commanded by Colonel William Washington, obtained the surrender of a Loyalist force by guile. They used the Quaker gun trick, fabricating a cannon from a log. The approximate 100 Loyalists surrendered rather than be bombarded.

December-11-1780   *SC, Long Cane:* Patriot Colonels Elijah Clarke and James McCall led a force of 100 men to Long Cane. They were attacked by a large force of Provincials and Loyalist militia from Ninety Six. The Loyalists were commanded by Lieutenant Colonel Isaac Allen. The Patriots were driven back. Both Clarke and MaCall were wounded.

December-12-1780   *SC, Halfway Swamp:* Francis Marion, the "Swamp Fox," discovers that the British Major Robert McLeroth is moving approximately 200 recruits from Charleston to Winnsboro. McLeroth offers to have 20 men from each side engage in combat to decide the issue in a ploy for time. That night the British force skulks away, leaving their campfires burning to deceive the Americans.

December-27-1780   *SC:* Americans raided Hammond's Store (Williamson's Plantation). Patriot Brigadier General Daniel Morgan detached a force of approximately 275 dragoons under the command of Colonel William Washington to destroy a force of Loyalists terrorizing the countryside in the vincity of Fairpoint Creek. Without losing any of his force, William Washington killed or wounded 150 of the Loyalists and took 40 prisoners.

January-17-1781   *SC, Cowpens:* Brigadier General Daniel Morgan, his riflemen and the Patriot militia annihilated Lieutenant Colonel Banastre Tarleton and his forces. The great southern victory buoyed American forces. American forces numbered 1,025 men, with 12 killed, 60 wounded in action. British forces numbered 1,100 men, with 100 killed, 229 wounded in action and 829 captured.

January-24-1781   *SC, Georgetown:* Patriot commanders Francis Marion and Henry Lee combined their forces and conducted a raid on Georgetown, which was defended by 200 British soldiers commanded by Colonel Archibald Campbell. The British troops refused to engage, the Americans paroled Campbell and his men.

January-31-1781   *SC, Wadboo Bridge:* After the unsatisfying raid on Georgetown of January 24–25, Brigadier General Francis Marion sent out several patrols to seek out and destroy, if possible, as many British supply bases/posts as they could. Captain John Postell, Jr. and his men destroyed the stores at Wadboo Bridge, including fifteen hogsheads of rum, a quantity of pork, flour, rice, salt, and turpentine.

February-19-1781   *SC, Fort Granby:* Patriot General Thomas Sumter laid a siege to Fort Granby under the command of Major Andrew Maxwell. The siege was broken when news of reinforcement was received. The siege lasted until 21 February.

March-1-1781   **SC, Fort Watson:** Needing supplies Brigadier Thomas Sumter and his Patriot force of over 200 men, decided to attack Fort Watson. Major John Harrison and his South Carolina Rangers drove Sumter and his men off. When the Patriots attacked the fort Lieutenant Colonel Tadwell-Watson commanded the fort. The Patriots suffered considerable casualties, 18 killed and 38 wounded in action.

March-6-1781   **SC, Wyboo Swamp:** Colonel John Watson was commanding a British column in pursuit of General Francis "Swamp Fox" Marion and his Patriot force. At Wyboo Swamp a Patriot soldier single handedly held a narrow causeway to give the Patriots time to withdraw.

March-29-1781   *SC, Snow's Island:* British Colonel Welborne Doyle carried out a pincer movement against Francis Marion's headquarters at Snow Island. After a brief skirmish Doyle captured the island. The island defenders commanded by Colonel Hugh Ervin, destroyed all the carefully hoarded supplies and ammunition before he abandoned the position.

April-15-1781   *SC, Fort Watson:* The siege of Fort Watson lasted from April 15 to April 25. The American force was led by General Francis "Swamp Fox" Marion with 80 men. The British force was led by Lieutenant McKay with 120 men. When Hezekiah Maham proposed building a tower, it was completed in five days and allowed the Patriots to fire down into the compound. Conclusion: an American victory.

April-25-1781 _SC, Hobkirk Hill:_ British won another victory near Camden. Even as General Nathaniel Greene retreated here, and was losing all battles, he was winning the southern campaign. General Nathaniel Greene was credited as saying, "We fight, get beat, rise and fight again." American forces had 1,551 men, with 19 killed, 115 wounded in action. British forces under Lieutenant Colonel Lord Rawden had a force of 900 men, with 38 killed, 170 wounded in action and 50 captured.

May-8-1781 _SC, Fort Motte:_ Siege of Fort Motte. American forces under General Francis Marion had 450 men with 2 killed in action. British troops were under the command of Lieutenant Colonel Donald McPherson with 175 men. The siege lasted 4 days when the Americans fired flaming arrows into the compound. The garrison surrendered. Conclusion: an American victory.

May-10-1781 _SC, Camden:_ The British abandon Camden, burning the town down so the Patriot forces behind them are unable to use the town as a supply stop.

May-15-1781 **SC, Fort Granby:** An American force commanded by Henry Lee assaulted a position commanded by Major Andrew Maxwell who had a Loyalist force of 352 men. Maxwell was well known for his plunder. After much haggling, Maxwell agreed to surrender if he was allowed to keep some of his plunder. It was agreed and the Patriots gained valuable ammunition and supplies. The Patriots won this without firing a shot.

May-21-1781 _SC, Fort Galphin:_ Lieutenant Colonel Henry Lee and his Legion were on their way to link up with militia forces besieging Augusta. Lee heard of a quantity of supplies stored at Fort Galphin, the supplies were the annual King's present to his loyal Indians. Lee upon reaching Fort Galphin was joined by some Georgia and South Carolina militia. Captain John Rudolph of Lee's Legion captured the fort and its supplies, which included blankets, clothing, small arms, ammunition, medical stores and provisions.

May-22-1781 _SC, Ninety Six:_ American forces, under Major general Nathanael Greene, have 185 men killed or wounded. The British under Colonel John Cruger, have 550 Loyalists, with 75 killed or wounded. Ninety Six was an important position in South Carolina. The Americans were unable to breech the line and retreated when they heard a rumor of reinforcements on the way. This siege lasts from May 22 to June 19.

SC, Saluda River: Lieutenant Colonel William Washington and his patriot force of dragoons surprised a group of Loyalist militia at the Saluda River, near Ninety Six and attacked. The Loyalists fled to Ninety Six.

July-16-1781 **SC, Biggin Church:** British Major Thomas Fraser was commanding a mounted unit of Loyalist South Carolina Rangers. They made a surprise attack on the Patriot camp of Major Generals Thomas Henry, Henry Lee, Francis Marion, Colonel Edward Lacey and his Patriot riflemen broke up the Loyalist attack. The Loyalists retreated.

July-17-1781 *SC, Quinby Bridge:* A combined Patriot force led by General Thomas Sumter with units from Henry Lee, Francis Marion, and Thomas Taylor meet a force commanded by Lieutenant Colonel John Coates holding an excellent defensive position. Sumter completely mismanaged the attack, and when 700 British reinforcements arrived the next day, the Americans broke off the engagement, Marion, Lee, and Taylor were so disgusted with Sumter they departed that day.

SC, Quinby Bridge: (Possibly August 17) A British force led by Lieutenant Colonel James Coates moved down the Cooper River, a Patriot force commanded by Brigadier General Thomas Sumter followed, after a few skirmishes the British surrendered. The American forces had 700 men, 30 killed and 30 wounded in action. The British had 600 men, 6 killed, 38 wounded in action and 100 captured.

August-4-1781 *SC:* Patriot militia officer Colonel Isaac Hayne is executed by the British. After Hayne was captured at Charlestown and paroled, the British attempted to have him join the Loyalist militia, but he refused. He then again joined the Patriots and was again captured, and executed.

August-13-1781 **SC, Parker's Ferry:** Patriot Colonel William Harden commanded a detachment of soldiers at Parker's Ferry. Loyalists numbering 450 men commenced an uprising and were to be reinforced by 200 dragoons, led by Major Thomas Fraser. The force moved undetected until it was ambushed by the Patriots. The Patriots severely mauled the dragoons. Only the shortage of ammunition saves the dragoons, who lost half their force.

August-30-1781 *SC, Parker's Ferry:* General Francis Marion set up an ambush at Parker's Ferry, at the site of Edisto River. A British force of dragoons was sent from Charleston to support the local Loyalist militia. The Dragoons entered the ambush site and half were either killed or wounded. The British casualties of a force of 200 were 100 killed or wounded.

September-8-1781 *SC, Eutaw Springs:* Battle of Eutaw Springs. Even though he was again defeated, General Nathanael Greene had been able to force the British back toward Charleston, regaining most of South Carolina. Greene had approximately 2,200 men while the British commander, Colonel Alexander Stewart had 2,000 men. The Patriots lost over 500 men, while the British lost almost 700 men killed or wounded. This was one of the last major engagements in the south.

September-28-1781 **VA:** Siege of Yorktown, combined forces under General George Washington and French General Rochambeau had an American force of 11,133 men, with 23 killed and 65 wounded in action. The French had 7,800 men, with 60 killed and 193 wounded in action. British forces were under the command of Lieutenant General Charles Cornwallis with 8,885 men; 156 killed, 326 wounded in action, and 8,087 captured. The siege lasted from September 28 to October 19. Conclusion: American/French victory.

October-6-1781 **VA, Yorktown:** Heavy ordinance was brought ashore from the French fleet and placed in position in earthworks around Yorktown. Trenches were dug to within 600 yards of the British positions.

October-19-1781 *VA:* Battle of Yorktown. General Charles Cornwallis and 7,000 men surrendered to General Washington.

November-17-1781   *SC, Fair Lawn:* A Patriot force of 980 troops, led by Colonels Isaac Shelby and Hezekiah Maham arrived at the British post at Fair Lawn. They attacked one of the outbuildings, which turned out to be a hospital. The hospital offered no resistance and surrendered. The Patriots captured 300 weapons, some stores and 150 prisoners. The hospital was burned as the Patriots rode away.

December-1-1781   *SC, Dorchester:* After the Battle of Eutaw Springs, Nathanael Greene departed the area. British forces were now commanded by John Doyle who took over for the wounded Alexander Stewart. Greene started an assault on Dorchester, which was defended by 850 men. The British failed to realize that Greene only had 400 men. The British, after destroying their provisions, made a hasty retreat to Charleston. The British were so concerned about the attack on the city that they armed black slaves.

January-1-1782   *SC, Jacksonborough:* After a two-year hiatus caused by war, the General Assembly met at Jacksonborough, a small town on the Edisto River about thirty miles from British-occupied Charleston. John Matthews was elected by the Jacksonborough Assembly on January 31, 1782, as South Carolina's second Governor, succeeding John Rutledge.

January-3-1782   *SC, Videau's Bridge:* British Major William Brereton, who commanded a force of 300 men arrived at Brabant Plantation, he rested his troops and posted guards at Videau's Bridge. Colonel Richard Richardson, Jr. led his men to the area and circled the bridge. The Patriots charged the British and sent them running. At the bridge the British fired a volley, and sent the Patriots off. The British pursued for 6 miles before turning back.

February-24-1782   *SC, Wambaw Bridge:* General Marion's Brigade under Colonel Archibald McDonald with about 500 men were defeated by Loyalist Colonel Benjamin Thompson with about 700 men and a 3-pound cannon.

May-28-1782   **SC, Dorchester:** A Patriot cavalry, commanded by Lieutenant Colonel John Laurens discovered a Loyalist force, commanded by Captain George Dawkins, at Dorchester. Laurens attacked and quickly defeated the Royalists.

August-7-1782   **NY:** General Washington established the "Badge of Merit" later referred to as the Purple Heart. It was originally awarded for singular meritorious action. The original medal was awarded to only three men: Sergeant Daniel Bissell, 2nd Connecticut Regiment, Sergeant William Brown, 5th Connecticut Regiment and Sergeant Elijah Churchill, 2nd Continental Dragoons. The medal was revived on February 22, 1932 by General Douglas Macarthur, and given to those wounded in combat. The Purple Heart is America's oldest military medal and has been awarded to over 1,000,000 recipients.

August-27-1782   **_SC, Combahee:_** Late in the war, a combined force of British regulars and Loyalists were trying to obtain forage for Charleston. Upon discovering the British intentions, the Patriots sent a force commanded by Colonel John Laurens to intercept them. Laurens and his men were ambushed, resulting in the death of Laurens and one other man.

August-29-1782   **_SC, Fair Lawn:_** An American force commanded by General Francis Marion had set up an ambush for an approaching British force of 200 dragoons, led by Major Thomas Fraser. After entering the ambush the British force lost 20 men killed in action, but Fraser captured Marion's ammunition wagon, which turned the tide of battle, Marion was forced to withdraw due to the lack of ammunition.

September-3-1782   **France, Paris:** Peace negotiations commenced in Paris. There were nine articles including, recognition of the 13 colonies, free navigation of the Mississippi River, fishing rights off the Grand Banks, and removal of all the British troops from American soil.

November-14-1782   **_SC, James Island:_** American Colonel Count Thaddeus Kosciuszko and his force of 70 Patriots engaged the British escort of a woodcutting party on James Island. British forces were quickly brought forward and greatly outnumbered the Patriots. The Patriots withdrew, its known as the last engagement in South Carolina.

December-14-1782   **_SC, Charleston:_** British forces evacuated Charleston. Major General Alexander Leslie, commanding British troops in South Carolina, withdrew his troops from Charleston. Along with the troops were 3,580 Loyalists and 500 enslaved people. At 10 AM after the British evacuated, Brigadier General Anthony Wayne and his Continental troops occupied the city.

January-1-1783 **NY:** Noah Webster's. "The American Spelling Book" standardized pronunciation and spelling, separated the American English from British English, and united America through the powerful medium of common language.

Canada: 100,000 Loyalists immigrated to Canada.

January-20-1783 **England, London:** Britain signed a peace agreement with France and Spain.

February-1-1783 **Europe:** Spain, Sweden, and Denmark recognized the independence of the United States of America.

April-15-1783 **PA, Philadelphia:** Congress ratified the preliminary peace treaty signed in November 1782.

April-19-1783 **NY:** General George Washington informed his troops that the war was over.

September-3-1783 **France, Paris:** The Peace Treaty was formally signed in Paris. Benjamin Franklin, John Adams and John Jay signed for the United States.

December-4-1783 **NY, NYC:** In a heartfelt gathering at Fraunces Tavern, General Washington took leave of his officers with a magnificent toast and tearfully embraced each one.

December-23-1783 **MD, Annapolis:** In another tear-filled gathering, Washington resigned his commission before Congress, "Commending the interests of our dear country to the protection of the Almighty God."

December-30-1783 **PA:** The first map of the United States was produced.

USA: During the Revolutionary War 231,771 soldiers served in the Continental Army, approximately 145,000 served in militia. Casualties were

4,435 killed and 6,118 wounded in action. Population of the US was approximately 2.1 million. It is estimated that over 35,000 men died from disease including dysentery, smallpox, venereal disease, typhoid and typhus and, in the south, malaria and fever.

Colonies: British troops in the colonies never exceeded 22,000 at any time.

Colonies: Loyalists numbered approximately 50,000 in the 8 years.

December-31-1783 **Colonies:** During the American Revolution, there were 1,331 military engagements and 315 naval actions.

Colonies: Estimates of soldiers by states:

Armies of the American Revolution

State	Continental Army	Military Militia	Total
NH	12,497	4,000	16,497
MA	67,907	20,000	87,907
RI	5,908	4,000	9,908
CT	31,939	9,000	40,939
NY	17,781	10,000	27,781
NJ	10,726	7,000	17,726
PA	25,678	10,000	35,678
DE	2,386	1,000	3,386
MD	13,912	9,000	22,912
VA	26,678	30,000	56,678
NC	7,263	13,000	20,263
SC	6,417	20,000	26,417
GA	2,679	8,000	10,679
	231,771	145,000	376,771

Simplified Chronological Order of Events

February-10-1763 — The treaty of Paris ends the French & Indian War. While Great Britain won the war, she was left with a lot of debt. Great Britain looks to the colonies for revenue to pay current debt and provide for future colonial protection.

April-5-1764 — Sugar Act requires regulation and duties on sugar and molasses.

March-22-1765 — Stamp Act places a tax on printed material and documents.

June-29-1767 — Townshend Revenue Acts create new import duties for colonies.

March-5-1770 — "Boston Massacre": King's troops kill five civilians in Boston, MA.

December-3-1773 — Charleston's first Tea Party.

December-16-1773 — Chests of tea destroyed in protest at "Boston Tea Party."

September-October-1774 — First Continental Congress meets in Philadelphia, PA. The "Minute Man" companies are formed and there are calls for a strong colonial union.

April-19-1775 — Battles of Lexington & Concord, MA. The first official shots were exchanged to start the war.

May-June-1775 — Second Continental Congress meets in Philadelphia, PA. Congress forms the Continental Army and George Washington is placed as Commander-in-Chief.

June-1775 — Lord William Campbell was appointed the Royal Governor of South Carolina.

September-15-1775 — The royal Governor, Lord William Campbell dissolved the General Assembly—South Carolina's ruling body and government.

November-1-1775 South Carolina establishes a Provincial Congress and commences meeting on this date.

March-4-1776 The committee submitted a draft of a constitution to the Provincial Congress for South Carolina.

March-26-1776 South Carolina became the first colony to establish a constitution. This constitution became a model for many of the other colonies.

May-2-1776 French Government sends $1 million worth of arms to the colonies.

May-10-1776 Continental Congress authorizes each of the 13 colonies to form new state governments.

June-19-28-1776 Great Britain planned to take Charleston by a simultaneous attack by land at Breach Inlet and Fort Sullivan by sea.

July-4-1776 Congress adopts the Declaration of Independence after a unanimous vote.

July-27-1777 Marquis de Lafayette arrives in Philadelphia, PA to volunteer for the American cause.

November-15-1777 Articles of Confederation adopted by Continental Congress. It was an agreement among the 13 original states that served as our first constitution.

February-23-1778 Baron von Steuben arrives at Valley Forge to begin a training program.

December-29-1778 Savannah, GA was captured by the British.

1779 The war spreads across the globe. Spain entered the war as an ally of France and soon declared war on Great Britain.

January-9-1779 John Rutledge was elected governor under the revised new state constitution.

May-7-1780   <u>Powder Magazine</u>: After near disaster when a British shell hit nearby on May 7, Gen. Moultrie emptied the Powder Magazine and moved the 100,000 pounds to two different locations on the outskirts of the city days before the city was surrendered to the British. The British never found what Gen. Moultrie hid and the old Powder Magazine is now completely renovated in Charleston.

1780   Two major defeats in South Carolina: <u>The capture of Charleston and the loss at Camden</u>. Yet the "tide turns" for the Patriots with the help of the "Overmountain Men" with a victory at Kings Mountain.

January-1781   Overmountain Men and militia help secure a <u>victory at Cowpens</u>.

October-19-1781   Major Gen. Nathanael Greene's masterful strategies as well as Franco-American cooperation secures victory in the South. After Greene frustrated Gen. Lord Cornwallis in the Carolinas, the British moved to Virginia where the Allies trapped his army. Thus leading to the end of the war. <u>Gen. Lord Cornwallis surrendered in Yorktown, VA on this day</u>.

1781-1782   <u>Continued fighting throughout South Carolina</u>.

September-3-1783   <u>Final peace treaty between Great Britain and the United States signed in Paris</u>. We, the United States of America, become a separate country/nation.

February-11-1785   <u>Gen. William Moultrie becomes Governor Moultrie</u> of South Carolina.

1786   <u>Capital of South Carolina moved</u> to Columbia from Charleston.

How to Use the Book & Page Setup

Region Name
Region # Site #

Marker	*
Gravesite/Monument	🪦
Liberty Trail App Site	🌙
Museum/Visitor Center	🏠
Open Field	🌾
Private Property/Do Not Enter	▦
Ruins	🏚

Site Name *Site has a marker

Date of Event

GPS Coordinates

County Location

Result: Who won the battle or skirmish

Combatants (Who fought)

Commanders and Leaders involved

Strength (number of soldiers and militia)

Casualties and Losses

Explanation of battle/ skirmish/ site.

What is written on the Marker

Date visited: _____

Comments about the site: _____

_____

_____

Midlands Region

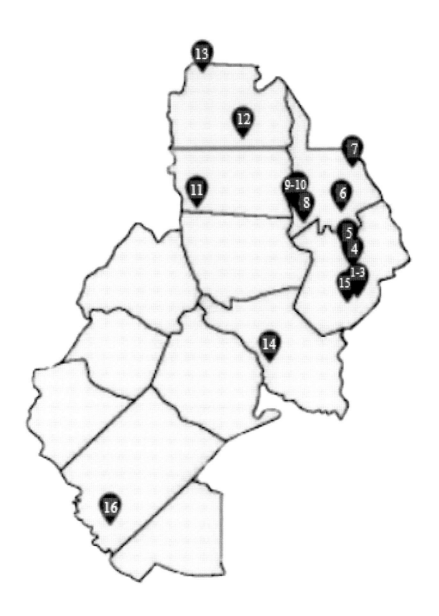

Midlands
Region 1

#	Location	County	Date
1.	Rev War Center-Camden	Kershaw	
2.	Camen-Occupied*	Kershaw	June 1, 1780–May 10, 1781
3.	Battle of Hobkirk Hill*	Kershaw	April 25, 1781
4.	Battle of Camden*	Kershaw	August 16, 1780
5.	Battle of Rugeley's Fort	Kershaw	December 4, 1780
6.	Battle of Hanging Rock #1*		
	Battle of Hanging Rock #2*	Lancaster	July 30, 1780
			August 6, 1780
7.	Battle of Waxhaws* (Buford's Massacre)	Lancaster	May 29, 1780
8.	Battle of Rocky Mount	Fairfield	August 1, 1780
9.	Battle of Alexander's Old Fields*	Chester	June 6, 1780
10.	Battle of Fishing Creek*	Chester	August 18, 1780
11.	Battle of Fishdam Ford*	Chester	November 9, 1780
12.	Battle of Huck's Defeat* (Brattonsville)	York	July 12, 1780
13.	Battle of Kings Mountain*	York	October 7, 1780
14.	Siege of Fort Granby #1		
	Siege of Fort Granby #2	Lexington	February 19–21, 1781
			May 2–15,1781
15.	Battle of Cary's Fort*	Kershaw	August 15, 1780
16.	Surrender of Fort Galphin (Fort Dreadnaught)	Aiken	May 21, 1781

Midlands
Region 1 Site 1

Revolutionary War Visitor Center

34.23209°N 80.60515°W

simplyrevolutionary.com

Kershaw County

The Revolutionary War Visitor Center (Rev War Center) in Camden is the gateway of information to South Carolina's pivotal role in the American Revolution and the introduction of things to do and see in Camden-Kershaw County.

The Rev War Center at Camden is a destination for visiting, learning, gathering, and sharing. The complex is built on 3.4 acres and comprises three buildings, The Public House, Market Building, and Liberty Hall.

- The Public House replicates a historic local tavern. Here the museum features exhibits that tell the story of the Southern Campaign and South Carolina's important role.
- The Market Building is modeled on an old-style, open-air market that once stood across from the historic Robert Mills Courthouse. This is a beautiful gathering space and meeting venue.
- Liberty Hall is designed to accommodate large groups, private and corporate events, education symposiums, and more. It serves as a space for learning, sharing, and gathering.

Date visited: _____

Comments: _____

_____

_____

Midlands
Region 1 Site 2

Camden—Occupied

34.23326°N 80.60408°W

June 1, 1780–May 10, 1781

historiccamden.org

Kershaw County

The Historic Camden Foundation is a museum whose mission is to protect, educate, and celebrate Camden's extraordinary colonial and Revolutionary War history.

The 103 acres is located on the original 18th century property of the city's founding father, Joseph Kershaw. After capturing Charleston in May 1780, British forces under General Charles Lord Cornwallis established a supply depot at Camden as part of their effort to control the South Carolina backcountry. The fortified Revolutionary-era town was occupied by British General Cornwallis from June, 1780–May, 1781. Visit this site to learn Camden's importance to the Revolutionary War and colonial life in the backcountry.

Historic Camden recently received ownership of the 476 acres of the Battlefield of Camden. It is hallowed ground. The Longleaf Pine forest is located at Region 1, Site 4.

*Marker
Historic Camden Revolutionary War Site:

Historic Camden Revolutionary War Site is located at the original site of Camden, the oldest inland town in South Carolina. Established in 1733, colonial Camden emerged as the trade center of the backcountry by the 1760s.

On June 1, 1780, Camden's citizens surrendered to General Charles, Lord Cornwallis and 2,500 British soldiers. For the next eleven months the garrisoned town served as the principal British inland post while the brutal 1780–81 Southern Campaign ravaged the Carolinas.

Two major battles were fought nearby: the Battle of Camden (August 1780) and the Battle of Hobkirk's Hill (April 1781). Commanders associated with Camden include American generals Horatio Gates, Nathanael Greene, and Baron Johann de Kalb, and British commanders Lord Cornwallis, Lord Rawdon and the infamous Banastre Tarleton.

The British burned most of the town when they evacuated in May 1781. Undaunted, the citizens rebuilt Camden just north of here.

This 107-acre museum includes five historic buildings, two of which contain exhibits, reconstructions of several British fortifications unearthed during archaeological investigations, and the reconstructed Kershaw mansion, which served as British headquarters.

Date visited: _____

Comments: _____

_____

_____

**Midlands
Region 1 Site 3**

Battle of Hobkirk Hill*
April 25, 1781

34.26669°N 80.60089°W

Kershaw County

Result: Tactical British victory
   Strategic American victory

Combatants	
Great Britain	United States
Loyalist militia	Patriot militia
Commanders and Leaders	
Col. Lord Rawdon	Maj. Gen. Nathanael Greene
Strength	
900	1,550
Casualties and Losses	
39 killed	21 killed
210 wounded	113 wounded
12 missing	47 captured
	89 missing

American Gen. Greene did not have enough troops to lay siege to the fortified town of Camden, so he hoped to provoke the South Carolina British commander, Lord Francis Rawdon, into an attack on his position. Col. Rawdon knew that if South Carolina militia Brig. Gen. Francis Marion and Lt. Col. Henry "Light Horse Harry" Lee joined Greene, Greene would have a superior force to his own. Rawdon's main supply and communication line to Nelson's Ferry (present day Orangeburg County) and Charleston had been severed by the fall of Fort Watson. Gen. Greene took every precaution to keep men from deserting, but in spite of this, a Maryland drummer named Jones did desert the night before the battle and informed Rawdon of Greene's weaknesses. Rawdon decided to attack and mustered everyone who could carry and fire a weapon, including his musicians, drummers, and walking wounded.

Rawdon silently formed his men at Little Pine Tree Creek and ordered a flanking advance on the Americans at 10 am. In the meantime, supplies and three cannons arrived at the American camp. Rawdon's attack commenced while the Americans were eating breakfast. However, the Americans were under arms at daylight and ready for the fight when Rawdon appeared. The British attacked the American pickets and the sound of the gunfire alerted the Americans who had time to form into a battle line just below the crest of Hobkirk Hill. The British emerged from the pine forest and formed a battle line extending west across the Great Waxhaws Road at the foot of Hobkirk Hill. Rawdon did not expect the Americans to have cannons due to the information supplied by the deserter, Jones. The American cannons quickly cleared the 90 foot wide road of the British causing many dead and wounded. Due to Rawdon's anger at this unexpected development, he ordered Jones to be hanged. Greene saw the British in trouble and pressed this attack by flanking the British on both sides and by ordering the cavalry to circle the battle to the east and come up behind the British. When Rawdon saw that he was about to be surrounded, he spread his line to stop the American's flanking and the fighting became intense. The British were able to counter-attack when the Americans fell into confusion from orders given by Col. John Gunby. Col. Gunby had ordered his 1st Maryland Regiment to fall back and reform after the 1st Maryland Regiment turned to the rear. The Americans began an organized retreat down the back (north side) of the hill. The Americans tried to regroup at the top of the hill, but it was too late. However, the Americans were able to save their cannons and ammunition as they retreated north about 4 miles. The British followed skirmishing with Greene's rear guard for 2½ miles, then returned to Camden. The battle only lasted about 20 minutes.

*Marker
Battle of Hobkirk Hill: in the Revolutionary War took place on this ridge April 25, 1781. The British Army was Commanded by General Lord Rawdon, the Continental Army by General Nathanael Greene.

Erected: 1956 by The Kershaw County Historical Society.

Date visited: _____

Comments: _____

_____

_____

Midlands
Region 1 Site 4

Battle of Camden*

August 16, 1780

4.35768°N 80.61029°W

Kershaw County

Result: British victory

Combatants	
Great Britain	United States
Loyalist militia	Patriot militia
Commanders and Leaders	
Lt. Gen. Lord Cornwallis	Maj. Gen. Horatio Gates
Col. Lord Rawdon	Maj. Gen. Johann DeKalb
	Col. Marquis de la Rouërie
Strength	
2,100	**4,000**
1,500 regulars	1,500 regulars
600 militia	2,500 militia
4 guns	8 guns
Casualties and Losses	
66 killed	900 killed and wounded
256 wounded	1,000 captured
11 missing	8 guns captured
	200+ wagons captured

The newly appointed Southern Department commander American Maj. Gen. Horatio Gates marched toward Camden from central North Carolina by a reasonably direct route. Lord Charles Cornwallis marched north from the British base at Camden to attack Gates in his camp at Rugeley's Mill. While Gates was moving his "Grand Army" toward his planned new camp north of Sanders Creek, out of the quiet of the night his advanced guard heard a sharp challenge and some scattered shots from the British vanguard. The advance troops of both armies came together at 2:30 in the morning on the Jasper Sutton farm just north of the ford over Gum Swamp about 8 miles north of Camden.

The British Legion cavalry dashed ahead to remove those that might block their path. American Lt. Col. Charles Tuffin Armand's cavalry withstood the charge for a few moments. Flanking columns of American infantry, under Maj. John Armstrong and Lt. Col. Charles Porterfield, then moved into position from which their fire struck the British Legion cavalry from both sides, causing its retreat.

Thus started the Battle of Camden. Both forces, moving at night, unexpectedly met in the dark on the road from Camden to Hanging Rock. Both armies halted as the wounded in both cavalries pulled back. The retreating corps moved into the front of the infantry columns behind. The 1st Maryland Continentals moved forward to support the American's advance guard of light infantry; they effectively held the ground thereby providing time for the units in the rear to establish battle order.

The prisoners taken by each side during the skirmish informed their captors of the "true" condition of the other side. Cornwallis was assured by both prisoners and deserters that the whole of Gates' army was marching with the intention of attacking the British at Camden and was far greater than his own. From one of the British who had been made a prisoner, Col. Otho Williams learned the startling information that 600 yards in front of the Americans lay the whole British Southern Army, consisting of about 3,000 regular troops commanded by Lord Charles Cornwallis himself. Both sides were astounded by this information. Each commander had to exercise prompt and heroic leadership to save his command from destruction and turn surprise into victory. First light was fast approaching and by 4:30 am, the dawn of day would bring the armies within sight of each other. Order was restored in the American corps of infantry and the officers formed their troops into a line of battle. Gates ordered Col. Williams to call a council of war with all the general officers, who immediately assembled in the rear and were told the unwelcome news of the enemy before them. Gen. Gates asked: "Gentlemen, what is best to be done?" All were silent for a few moments, then Brig. Gen. Edward Stevens exclaimed: "Is it not too late now to do anything but fight?"

The American line was from a low area on the west side of the road and extended about 1/3 mile across the Great Waxhaw Road (now the Flat Rock Road) to the east. Cornwallis described the battleground as "being narrowed by swamps on the right and left and was extremely favorable to my number." The British also formed their troops into a line of battle that extended about the same distance on both sides of the road. As dawn broke, American artillery officer, Capt. Anthony Singleton could see the British movements only 200 yards in front of him. An artillery exchange commenced that killed and wounded many on each side. The British regulars posted on the American right flank advanced towards the Virginia and North Carolina militia with bayonets. The Virginian and North Carolina militia fled, many without firing a shot.

Gates tried to rally the fleeing troops, but to no avail. As his left (east) flank collapsed, the Maryland and Delaware Continentals on the American right (west) flank held fast under Maj. Gen. Johann-Alexandre Von Robaii, "Baron" DeKalb. These 600 men stood against 2,000 British troops. DeKalb's horse was shot, but he continued to fight on foot. After being wounded by a sword slash to the head and having it bandaged, he grabbed his sword and led a counter attack that temporarily drove the British back, but put DeKalb in the middle of the British troops as they swept around his men pursuing the fleeing troops. He was now separated from the main American force by about 200 yards as the general fighting swayed back and forth several times. The Continentals fought on for 45 minutes. DeKalb was wounded 11 times in the fierce fighting and fell to the ground. His men saw him fall and also saw the charging British, and even though DeKalb was not dead, his men, now surrounded, surrendered or fled. DeKalb died in Camden three days later.

*Marker
BATTLE OF CAMDEN

Near here on August 16, 1780, an American army under General Gates was defeated by British forces commanded by Lord Cornwallis. Major General Baron de Kalb was mortally wounded in this battle.

Battle of Camden:

Near here on August 16, 1780, an American army under General Gates was defeated by British forces commanded by Lord Cornwallis. Major General Baron de Kalb was mortally wounded in this battle.

British Troops Engaged
Tarleton's Legion, Twenty-third, Thirty-third and Seventy-first Regiments, Volunteers of Ireland, Royal Artillery, four light infantry companies, Royal North Carolina Militia, volunteer militia, and pioneers.

American Troops Engaged
Armand's Legion, First and Second Maryland Brigades, Delaware Regiment, First Artillery Regiment, Poterfield's Light Infantry, North Carolina Militia, and Virginia Militia.

Erected: 1954 by The Kershaw County Historical Society.

Date visited: _____

Comments: _____

_____

_____

Longleaf at Battle Field

Historic Camden's longleaf pine preserve and battlefield demonstrates how longleaf promotes an open understory. One can imagine the ample room to face enemy lines—or run, when walking amongst trees. When the battle took place more than 240 years ago, it was likely the trees were 4 feet in diameter, 150 feet tall, and up to 400 years old—that's as tall as about 25 people and as wide as a park bench!

To learn more about the unique way Longleaf pine grows and adapts around fire, visit Historic Camden's Eagle Loop trail at the Longleaf Pine Preserve and Battle Field. The trail is an easy, flat, 10 minute walk amongst a growing and revitalized longleaf stand at the hallowed ground of the historic Battle of Camden site.

Date visited: _____

Comments: _____

_____

_____

Midlands
Region 1 Site 5

Battle of Rugeley's Fort

34.40804°N 80.64398°W

December 4, 1780

Kershaw County

Result: Patriot victory

Combatants	
Great Britain Loyalist militia	United States
Commanders and Leaders	
Col. Henry Rugeley	Lt. Col. Washington Brig. Gen. Daniel Morganouërie
Strength	
114	80
Casualties and Losses	
109 killed	unknown

Lt. Col. William Washington, operating his cavalry, about 3 miles in front of Gen. Daniel Morgan's light infantry, decided to make an attempt against the Loyalist post at Rugeley's Fort, about twelve miles north of Camden. This post was located on the plantation of Loyalist militia Col. Henry Rugeley that he had named "Clermont." The fortification was Rugeley's barn, built of strong logs with firing ports cut into the walls; a place was made on the second floor for musketry; and a strong abatis (sharpened trees or logs closely spaced pointing outward) surrounded the barn. It was impregnable to a detachment of cavalry not equipped with artillery, but Col. Washington was not discouraged. He mounted a pine log to look like a cannon. (This is known as a Quaker cannon.) Then sent a message to Rugeley demanding immediate surrender. Rugeley fell for the trick and surrendered. The next morning a patrol sent from Camden by British Lord Francis Rawdon found only the burning embers of the fort. As a result of his actions, Rugeley did not receive a promotion to brigadier general.

The Continentals soon learned of their new commanding officer, Major Gen. Nathanael Greene after this.

Date visited: _____

Comments: _____

_____

_____

Midlands
Region 1 Site 6

Battle of Hanging Rock*

 # 1 July 30, 1780   34.56565°N 80.66175°W

#2 August 6, 1780   34.57151°N 80.68041°W

Lancaster County

Result: Patriot victory

Combatants	
Great Britain Loyalist militia	Patriot militia
Commanders and Leaders	
Col. Samuel Bryan	Maj. William Richardson Davis
Strength	
500	80
Casualties and Losses	
0	0

Hanging Rock 1: July 30, 1780: The battle took place at a house. The units engaged were militia, both Loyalist and Patriot, most from Mecklenburg County, NC. About 1,000 British were posted in several camps within .5 miles of each other. This attack was a diversion to keep the British at Hanging Rock from going to the aid of those under siege at the British post at Rocky Mount, then under attack by Patriot Col. Thomas Sumter. About 80 patriots under Maj. William Richardson Davie rode into the yard of a farmhouse where Col. Samuel Bryan's North Carolina Loyalist militia were having breakfast after a patrol. They easily passed the pickets since they looked just like the Loyalist militiamen. When the Loyalists tried to escape the house, riflemen, stationed to fire on the front yard, killed many Tories. The Patriots took horses and arms, but no prisoners, since those still alive, fled.

Result: Patriot victory

Combatants	
Great Britain Loyalist militia	Patriot militia
Commanders and Leaders	
Maj. John Carden	Brig. Gen Thomas Sumter
Strength	
1,400	800
Casualties and Losses	
25 killed 175 wounded	12 killed 41 wounded

Hanging Rock #2: August 6, 1780: Seven days later, on August 6, 1780, the second battle also began at daybreak, at Col. Bryan's camp due to a mistake by the guides employed by the Patriot Commander, Col. Thomas Sumter. This proved to be a blessing, as a frontal attack would not have succeeded against the 1,000 or so Loyalist militia and regular British troops that were camped by units in a line between the beginning and ending locations. This battle lasted 3.5 hours. Sumter attacked three divisions with most of it hand to hand combat as the Patriots had no uniforms and were dressed alike, except that the Patriots had a white piece of paper stuck in their hats to identify themselves to their comrades. Eight hundred Patriots successfully defeated the British troops and militia, capturing much needed supplies of horses, arms, powder, etc. The remaining British and Loyalists assumed a defensive square in the area of the house on the west side of the road. The Patriots broke off the engagement as they had as many supplies as they could carry, and received a false report of enemy reinforcements being within 0.5 hour march of the battle. One British regiment was so decimated that it never entered into another battle during the war.

*Marker

Battle of Hanging Rock:

About 2.5 miles south is Hanging Rock, where Maj. Davie surprised a British force, Aug. 1, 1780, and killed or wounded most of them. There also, Aug. 6, 1780, Col. Hill, Col. Irwin, and Maj. Davie, all under Gen. Sumter, successfully attacked the Prince of Wales's American Regiment and detachments of the 63rd and of the 71st Infantries, under Maj. Carden.

Erected: 1941 by Lancaster County.

The Battle Of The Hanging Rock:

Here was fought the Battle of the Hanging Rock August 6, 1780

About 600 Militia of the Carolinas under Colonel Thomas Sumter destroyed the British Camp and killed and wounded over 200 of the British Troops under Major John Carden with a loss of 40 killed and a few wounded.

Date visited: _____

Comments: _____

_____

_____

Midlands
Region 1 Site 7

Battle of the Waxhaws*
(Buford's Massacre)
May 29, 1780

34.74189°N 80.62587°W

Lancaster County

Result: British victory

Combatants	
Great Britain Loyalist militia	United States

Commanders and Leaders	
Lt. Col. Banastre Tarleton	Col. Abraham Buford

Strength	
150 dragoons and mounted cavalry	**420 total** 380 infantry 40 dragoons

Casualties and Losses	
5 killed 12 wounded	113 killed 150 wounded and paroled 53 captured

After the fall of Charleston, the only regiment of Continental troops within South Carolina was commanded by Col. Abraham Buford, who had arrived from Virginia with reinforcements too late to join the garrison at Charleston. Buford's troops retreated northward from the Santee River. Lt. Col. Banastre Tarleton was sent in pursuit by Lord Cornwallis and was able to overtake Buford on May 29, 1780, near the Waxhaws settlement. The ground on which Buford was forced to make his stand was not well suited for defense against cavalry. Soon after the commencement of the battle, Buford ordered his troops to surrender, realizing that further resistance was useless. Tarleton's dragoons ignored the flag of truce and continued to slaughter the American troops. The battle is variously known as Buford's Massacre, Buford's Defeat, or the Battle of the Waxhaws. The massacre of Buford's men aroused a spirit of revenge among many backcountry Patriots. From this time forward, "Tarleton's Quarter" meant giving no quarter by the Patriots to surrendering British. Tarleton had achieved his objective; South Carolina was now free of any Continental military to give resistance to Royal authority. The purpose of the British campaign was the restoration of South Carolina's allegiance to the crown, considered from this standpoint, the Waxhaws' Massacre was a disaster. Buford's defeat and the harsh treatment that many South Carolinians received at the hands of the British would soon result in the appearance of partisan militia bands intent on continuing the struggle against British rule.

*Marker
BUFORD'S BLOODY BATTLEGROUND
Col. Buford's 11th Virginia Regiment and a detachment of Washington's Calvary. Retreating after the fall of Charles Town, they were attacked by Col. Tarleton. May 29, 1780, at the site of the monument 955 feet southwest. The American loss was 113 killed. 150 wounded. 53 made prisoners: The British, 5 killed, 14 wounded. In that grave lie many of Col. Buford's men.

Battle of the Waxhaws: Massacre or Myth?
Immediately after the engagement, reports spread that many were stabbed and killed as they tried to surrender. Many were taken to a local Presbyterian church where local residents cared for them, including a young Andrew Jackson and his mother. Banastre Tarleton was denounced and over time became known as "Bloody Ban the Butcher" for his actions on the battlefield. In his report to the Virginia Assembly, Colonel Buford confirmed that "Our loss is very great… many of which (were) killed after they had laid down their arms." For his part, Tarleton acknowledged an erroneous report that he had been slain "stimulated the soldiers to a vindictive asperity not easily restrained." While historians continue to debate the events that occurred at the Waxhaws, it is clear that Tarleton's actions, here and elsewhere, stirred and angered the backcountry settlers into action.

The Spark to Independence
After the surrender of Charleston in May 1780, all organized Patriot resistance in the South was nearly extinguished. However, the British followed their victory with heavy-handed treatment of the rural population.

Battle of the Waxhaws: Massacre or Myth? Marker
General Clinton proclaimed that those who did not take an oath to the King would be treated as "rebels and enemies to their country." None could remain neutral. Throughout the Carolinas, the conflict disintegrated into terrible civil war. Loyalists sought vengeance on their beaten Patriot neighbors. Patriot militia rallied and treated Loyalists in a like manner. As the

British Legion burned and pillaged the countryside, stories were told and retold of the slaughter at the Waxhaws. Indeed, the phrase "Tarleton's Quarter" became synonymous with cruel treatment and the execution of prisoners.

Buford's Massacre May 29, 1780
On this site, Col. Abraham Buford's force of about 350 American patriots, while returning to Hillsborough, N.C., following the fall of Charles Town, were overtaken by British troops commanded by Col. Banastre Tarelton, it is historically told that the patriots white flag of surrender was disregarded as Tarelton's forces massacred the Americans. 113 patriots killed and buried here in mass graves, 150 wounded, most of whom died within a few days, 53 captured, and only a few escaped on horse back from this battle came the war cry "Remember Tarelton's Quarter." This monument is dedicated to the honored memory of the men who fought and died for our independence. This 29th day of May 2005, the 225th anniversary of the battle.

Erected: 2005.

Buford's Defeat

1. Buford's Defeat Marker

Tarleton's Ploy
After leaving General Cornwallis' army on May 27, Tarleton drove his men and horses relentlessly, covering 105 miles in 54 hours. He sent a messenger ahead with a surrender demand. Colonel Buford refused.

Tarleton's ploy delayed the Virginians long enough to allow the British advance guard to catch up with and capture Buford's rear guard, consisting of only five men. Colonel Buford sent his wagons, baggage, and artillery ahead and chose his defensive position: a single defensive line "in an open wood to the right of the road."

At a distance of three hundred yards, Tarleton halted and formed a reserve "upon a small eminence that commanded the road."

He divided his force into three groups to simultaneously attack Buford's left, center, and right; Tarleton led the assault on the left flank.

Buford's Folly

Buford ordered his line to withhold their fire until the charging cavalrymen were only at ten yards distance. The tactic was a serious mistake. The horsemen immediately overran Buford's line. Tarleton was shot off his horse. Loyalists sabered and bayoneted the Continentals; some tried to surrender, waving white flags, others fought stubbornly, and a few fled. Colonel Buford escaped on horseback.

British casualties were minimal—only five killed and fourteen wounded, while American losses were substantial—113 killed, 150 wounded (many of whom later died), and 53 taken prisoner.

From map insets:

Buford's Command:
- 350 Virginia Continentals of the Third Provisional Regiment,
- 40 Virginia Light Dragoons,
- Two six-pounder guns and crews.

Tarleton's Command:
- 130 British Legion cavalrymen,
- 100 mounted Legion infantrymen,
- a 40-man detachment of the 17th Light Dragoons,
- a 3 pounder field gun and crew.

Buford Monument

1. Buford Monument
(South Face of Monument)

Erected to the memory and in honor of the brave and patriotic American soldiers who fell in the battle which occurred at this place on the 29th May 1780 between Col. Abraham Buford who commanded a regiment of 350 Virginians and Col. Tarleton of the British Army with 350 Cavalry and a like number of Infantry.

(East Face of Monument)

Nearly the entire command of Col. Buford was either killed or wounded, 84 gallant soldiers are buried in this grave. They left their homes for the relief of Charleston, but hearing at

Camden of the surrender of that city, were returning. Here their lives were ended in the service of their country.

(North Face of Monument)

The cruelty and barbarous massacre committed on this occasion by Tarleton and his command after the surrender of Col. Buford and his regiment, originated the American war cry, "Remember Tarleton's Quarter." A British historian confesses at this battle "The virtue of humanity was totally forgot."

Erected: 1860.

Buford Battleground

In order that all may continue to share the sentiments of that group of patriotic citizens of Lancaster County who erected a monument here on June 2, 1860 the inscriptions of this memorial are the same as those on the original monument.

Erected to the memory and in honor of the brave and patriotic American soldiers who fell in the battle which occurred at this place on the 29th of May, 1780 between Col. Abraham Buford who commanded a regiment of 350 Virginians and Col. Tarelton of the British Army with 350 cavalry and a like number of infantry.

Nearly the entire command of Col. Buford were either killed or wounded. Gallant soldiers are buried in this grave that left their homes for the relief of Charleston, hearing at Camden of the surrender of that city were returning. Here their lives were ended in the service of their country. The cruelty and barbarous massacre committed on this occasion by Tarleton and his command after the surrender of Col. Buford and his regiment originated the war cry "Remember Tarleton's Quarters" a British historian confesses.

2. Buford Battleground Marker

at this battle the virtue of humanity was totally forgot.

Erected: 1955 by Waxhaw Chapter—Daughters of the American Revolution and the Lancaster County Historical Commission.

Date visited: _____

Comments: _____

_____

_____

Midlands
Region 1 Site 8

Battle of Rocky Mount

August 1, 1780

34.53643°N 80.88478°W

Fairfield County

Result: Loyalist victory

Combatants	
Loyalist militia	Patriot militia
Commanders and Leaders	
Lt. Col. George Turnbull	Brig. Gen Thomas Sumter
Strength	
300	500
Casualties and Losses	
20 killed and wounded	12 killed and wounded

The British at Rocky Mount were in two fortified buildings that were standing about 100 feet or so from the old road leading to the ferry over the Catawba River to Hanging Rock, 16 miles away. These two outposts constantly patrolled the road and supported each other if attacked. To provide a diversion prior to the attack on Rocky Mount, South Carolina Patriot militia Col. Thomas Sumter sent Maj. William R. Davie with 80 mounted men to attack Hanging Rock. This kept the British at Hanging Rock occupied while Sumter attacked Rocky Mount. Davie's men were successful in their attack.

Sumter and the Patriots at Rocky Mount could not execute the attack as planned since the gunfire from the fortified house was too heavy. Two volunteers agreed to run the 100 feet or so, under heavy fire, to throw burning lighter wood bundles in an attempt to burn the fort. However, the heavy rain prevented the success of the plan. With no hope of dislodging the British at Rocky Mount, the Americans withdrew.

Date visited: _____

Comments: _____

_____

_____

Midlands
Region 1 Site 9

Battle at Alexander's Old Fields*

34.59065°N 80.92006°W

(Battle of Beckhamville)
June 6, 1780

Chester County

Result: Patriot victory

Combatants	
Loyalist militia	Patriot militia
Commanders and Leaders	
Col. Housman	Capt. John McClure
Strength	
200	33
Casualties and Losses	
12 killed and wounded	20 killed and wounded

Patriot militia Capt. John McClure collected a party of 33 Patriot militia and attacked a group of Loyalists gathering to take British protection at Alexander's Old Fields. The Loyalists were commanded by a Capt. Housman, and numbered about two hundred. They were surprised, defeated, and dispersed by this small Patriot force. It was the first Patriot victory in South Carolina after the fall of Charleston and the beginning of a great wave of Carolina Backcountry resistance to the British and their Tory allies.

*Marker
BATTLE OF BECKHAMVILLE
May 1780
British under Houseman surprised and defeated by band of 33 Patriots under Capt. John McLure with 9 Gaston Brothers and neighbors, who struck first blow for liberty and resisted attempt to subject people to oath of allegiance to King. Erected by citizens of Chester Co. and Mary Adair Chapter DAR May 10, 1942.

Alexander's Old Fields

The skirmish which took place here at Alexander's Old Fields, now Beckhamville, on June 6, 1780, was the first victory for S.C. Patriots after the fall of Charleston. A band of Whigs under the command of Captain John McClure attacked and routed an assembly of Loyalist. The victory helped solidify resistance to the Crown in this up country area.

Erected: 1978 by Chester County Historical Society.

Date visited: _____

Comments: _____

_____

_____

Midlands
Region 1 Site 10

Battle of Fishing Creek*

August 18, 1780

34.63500°N 80.90417°W

Chester County

Result: British victory

Combatants	
Great Britain Loyalist militia	United States
Commanders and Leaders	
Lt. Col. Banastre Tarleton	Brig. Gen. Thomas Sumter
Strength	
160 regulars and militia	100 regulars 700 militia 2 cannons
Casualties and Losses	
16 killed and wounded	150+ killed 300 captured

The Battle of Fishing Creek was also known as the Battle of Catawba Ford/ Sumter's Defeat/ War on Sugar Creek. It was fought near the junction of Fishing Creek and the Catawba River in South Carolina.

British forces under Lieutenant Colonel Banastre Tarleton surprised the militia company of Thomas Sumter, killing a significant number, taking about 300 captives, and very nearly capturing Sumter.

***Marker**

BATTLE OF FISHING CREEK

At this site on August 18, 1780 General Thomas Sumter camped with captured booty and 800 men. He was surprised and defeated by Lt. Col. Tarleton and 160 soldiers. The disaster followed by only two days General Gates's defeat by Lord Cornwallis at Camden. The patriots lost 150 men killed and many captured, but Sumter escaped and soon rallied another large force.

Erected: 1974 by Chester County Historical Society.

Date visited: _____

Comments: _____

_____

_____

Midlands
Region 1 Site 11

Battle of Fishdam Ford*

34.59444°N 81.41611°W

November 9, 1780

Chester/Union County

Result: Patriot victory

Combatants	
Great Britain	United States
Commanders and Leaders	
Maj. James Wemyss	Brig. Gen. Thomas Sumter
Strength	
210 regulars	525 militia
40 militia dragoons	
Casualties and Losses	
16 killed and wounded	unknown

This action is shown in Chester County because that is where modern historians and archaeology tell us it happened. The historical marker gives a brief account of the action, but Rev. James Hodge Saye, *Memoirs of Major Joseph McJunkin—Revolutionary Patriot*, 1847, gives the following account.

"Historians generally state that Sumter's camp was on the east side of the river; this is a mistake. His position was west of Broad River, and his camp midway between that stream and a small creek which, flowing from the west, falls into the river near a mile below the ford. Here, says local tradition, was Sumter's camp. The whole selection between the streams is now cleared and under cultivation, and is entirely overlooked by a high ridge, along which the road leading from Hamilton's Ford to the Fishdam passed. It is presumed that the road was then very near where it now is. About half a mile from the creek a road leading from the mouth of Tyger River intercepts the one leading from Hamilton's Ford. A traveler approaching the ford by this route has a fine view of Sumter's position as he descends the long hill before reaching the creek.

"Again, says local tradition, on the night of Nov. 12 the fires were kindled in Sumter's camp at dark, and the soldiers began to divert themselves in various ways, apparently as devoid of care as a company of wagoneers occupying the same spot for the night would be at the present day. No special pains were taken by the general to have guards placed.

"But one officer in the camp was oppressed by anxious solicitude. That man was Col. Thomas Taylor of Congaree. He had been out with his command during a part of the previous day toward the Tyger River. In his excursions he had heard of the approach of the party under Wemyss, and from his intelligence of their movements he conjectured their purpose. He went to Sumter and demonstrated in regard to the state of things in his camp. Sumter gave him the understanding that he feared no danger, and felt prepared for any probable result. Taylor's apprehensions were not allayed by the security of his commander. He was determined to take measures to guard against surprise, and to this Sumter gave his hearty assent. Taylor conjectured that if the enemy came that night his approach would be along the road leading from the mouth of the Tyger and hence must cross the creek at the ford to reach Sumter's position.

"He placed himself at the head of his own men, marched them across the creek, built up large fires of durable material, sent out a patrol party in the direction of the enemy, examined a way for a safe retreat for his party down the creek, and took all other precautions deemed proper in the circumstances. He withdrew his men from the fires some distance in the direction of the main army and directed them what to do in case of alarm.

"They slept on their arms until midnight, when they were aroused by the fire of their sentinels. The patrol party had missed the enemy, and hence no alarm was given until the sentinels fired. The British, judging from the extent of Taylor's fire that the main body occupied that position and that no advance guard had been placed, immediately charged down the hill with the expectation of falling upon Sumter's men in confusion. They crowded around the blazing fires in search of their victims. Taylor's men were ready and delivered their fire at this juncture. The enemy fell back, but were again brought to the charge, but were again repulsed and fled in consternation, leaving their bleeding commander to the mercy of their foes.

"It is said that when Taylor's men delivered their first fire, a scene of confusion resulted in Sumter's camp utterly beyond description. The soldiers and officers ran hither and thither, whooping and yelling like maniacs. Some got ready for action and joined in it, while others ran clear off and did not join Sumter again for weeks. Hence this action was denominated in the region round about as "Sumter's Second Defeat," though the rout of the enemy was complete and the American loss was nothing."

*Marker

BATTLE OF FISHDAM FORD

On the east side of Broad River by an old Indian fish dam. General Thomas Sumter's camp was attacked by the British 63rd Regiment and a detachment of the Legion, led by Major James Wemyss. The American campfires made excellent targets of the mounted British, who were severely defeated. Wemyss was taken prisoner by General Sumter.

Erected: 1974 by Chester County Historical Society.

Erected by Chester Rotary Club 1928

To mark Fishdam Battle Ground Nov. 8. 1780 between

Gen. Sumter, American

Maj. Wemyss, British

Won by Americans

Date visited: _____

Comments: _____

_____

_____

Midlands
Region 1 Site 12

Battle of Huck's Defeat*

34.86484°N 81.17611°W

(Brattonsville)

July 12, 1780

York County

Result: Patriot victory

Combatants	
Great Britain Loyalist militia	Patriot militia
Commanders and Leaders	
Capt. Christian Huck	Lt. Col. William Bratton Lt. Col. William Hill Col. Edward Lacey Col. Andrew Neel Capt. James McClure
Strength	
35 dragoons 20 New York volunteers 50 militia	140
Casualties and Losses	
81 killed, captured, or wounded 24 escaped	1 killed 1 wounded

Loyalist Capt. Christian Huck of the British legion, on his march to put down the rebellion in the New Acquisition (York County), took 3 old men prisoners at South Carolina Patriot militia Col. William Bratton's home and Mrs. Bratton was forced to feed the invaders. Col. Bratton was away raising his militia to fight Huck. After eating, Huck moved ¼ mile east to camp for the night at Williamson's plantation, the residence of Patriot James Williamson. On July 12, in the early morning, Huck's cavalrymen were encircled by a split force of the Patriot troops numbering about 140 men from Thomas Sumter's camp under the command of South Carolina Patriot militia Cols. William Bratton, William Hill, Edward Lacey, Andrew Neel, and Capt. James McClure. The New York Volunteers, British Legion and South Carolina Loyalist militia were routed. This battle was the first in which South Carolina Patriot militia defeated trained British troops. After the battle, Loyalist Capt. Abraham Floyd's Rocky Mount Regiment switched to the cause of the Patriots, adding all their horses and equipment to the Patriot side and increased Sumter's ranks to 600 men.

*Marker
On July 12, 1780, at Williamson's Plantation about one-fifth of a mile east from here, Loyalist forces under Capt. Christian Huck were defeated by American forces led by Cols. William Bratton, William Hill, Edward Lacey, Richard Winn, as well as Captain John Moffett. Six months after this battle, known as "Huck's Defeat," came the pivotal American victories at Kings Mtn. in Oct. 1780 and Cowpens in Jan. 1781.

Field of Huck's Defeat
[Front Marker]
Where 75 Whigs led by
Colonel William Bratton
defeated a British and Tory
force of 500 men
July 12, 1780.

On this date, Sept.30, 1953, there stands 200 feet to the north of this stone, the Revolutionary home of Col. William Bratton and his wife, Martha. The land was a grant under George the Third.

[Rear Marker]
To the memory of
Mrs. Martha Bratton
wife of
Col. William Bratton

Loyal in the face of death.
Brave in the hour of danger.
Merciful in the moment of victory.

Erected: 1902 by Kings Mountain Chapter—Daughters of the American Revolution.
The Battle of Huck's Defeat
The information on the historical marker to the left[sic] is not accurate,

The inscription on the back is an honorable tribute to Martha Bratton's bravery prior to the battle. Watt's tombstone, a reproduction, is in tribute to his significant patriotic activities during the American Revolution.

In May of 1780, Charleston, South Carolina fell to the British who quickly overran much of the state. The only part of South Carolina to mount any sizable resistance to the British and Tory campaign was the area of present-day York and Chester Counties. Under the leadership of General Thomas Sumter, William Bratton and other men of this area formed militia companies. Colonel William Bratton became active in raids of British outposts and Tory meetings. Outraged at this interference with the submission of the state, the British sent a combined Provincial and Tory force to arrest Colonel Bratton.

Captain Christian Huck and about 130 men arrived at the Bratton home on the evening of July 11, 1780. Martha Bratton was questioned about the whereabouts of William Bratton. When Colonel Bratton received word from Watt, a Bratton slave, of Captain Huck's presence near his home, he hastened back with other militia regiments led by Colonels Hill, Lacey and McClure. Arriving early on the morning of July 12th, the patriot force of about 500 men found the Tories encamped at the Williamson farm nearby. During the night, the patriot forces surrounded the British encampment. The patriots opened fire at dawn, just as the British were rising from their bedrolls. Completely surprised and outnumbered, the British and Tory forces were unable to mount an effective counterattack. Captain Huck was killed during the battle.

Historians credit the victory at the battle of Huck's Defeat as the first link in the chain of events in the South that ultimately led to victory at Yorktown, Virginia. The Battle of Huck's Defeat, along with several other small battles in the area were important morale boosters for the patriots culminating in other American victories, such as the Battle of Kings Mountain.

William Bratton Plantation/Battle of Huck's Defeat
Side 1: William Bratton Plantation
In 1766 William Bratton and his wife Martha Robertson purchased 200 acres on the South Fork of Fishing Creek and built a single-pen log house here at the junction of several important

colonial roads. The Bratton home was the first in what would become the community of Brattonsville. Bratton was an important civil leader, serving also as an officer in the patriot militia during the Revolution.

Side 2: Battle of Huck's Defeat

James Williamson also settled on Fishing Creek in 1766 and built a log house 400 yards SE of here. On July 12, 1780, 120 British and loyalist troops, led by Christian Huck, camped at the Williamson home. They were attacked and defeated by 140 local patriot militiamen led by Colonel William Bratton and other officers in the Battle of Williamson's Plantation or "Huck's Defeat."

Erected: 2015 by Culture & Heritage Museum of York County.

Date visited: _____

Comments: _____

_____

_____

Midlands
Region 1 Site 13

Battle of Kings Mountain*

35.14125°N 81.37718°W

October 7, 1780

York County

Result: Patriot victory

Combatants	
Loyalist militia	Patriot militia

Commanders and Leaders	
Maj. Patrick Ferguson	Col. William Campbell
Capt. Abraham de Peyster	Capt. James Johnson
Col. Vezey Husbands	Lt. Col. John Sevier
Col. Ambrose Mills	Capt. Frederick Hambright
Maj. Daniel Plummer	Col. Joseph McDowell
	Col. Benjamin Cleveland
	Col. James Williams
	Col. Isaac Shelby
	Maj. Joseph Winston
	Maj. William Chronicle

Strength	
1,105	900

Casualties and Losses	
290 killed	28 killed
163 wounded	62 wounded
668 captured	

After the fall of Charleston, Patriots in Carolina backcountry continued fighting the British and local Loyalists. British Lord Cornwallis sent Maj. Patrick Ferguson to organize Loyalist militias to subdue the Carolina backcountry. While in North Carolina, Ferguson threatened to lay waste to the settlers west of the Blue Ridge with fire and sword, and hang their leaders should they continue to support the Patriot cause. These words were not taken lightly by the rugged Patriots in the mountains and they began to gather along what is known as the "Over Mountain Trail" that began in eastern Tennessee and ran through North Carolina into South Carolina. After joining with other Patriot militia forces from Virginia, South Carolina, and Georgia, the Patriots spent a number of days trying to find Ferguson. He was found camped on top of Kings Mountain, which had a flat top about 600 yards long and 40 yards wide that would accommodate his 1,125 men.

On October 7, armed with detailed information about Ferguson's camp provided by a released Patriot, 1,100 Americans silently surrounded Kings Mountain, trapping the British on the top. The battle started at 3 pm and raged for only a short time with the Americans moving up the steep slopes to the summit. They were forced back by British bayonet charges down the slopes (the Americans had no bayonets, as they could not be mounted on their rifles), so they gave way to the British. As the British charged down three different times, many died from rifle fire from behind the trees; then, as they retreated back up the slope, more were killed by American rifle fire. Patriot Capt. Moses Shelby was waged with tomahawks and knives. The Loyalists were finally pushed to one end of the mountain, completely surrounded by backwoodsmen, where two British officers attached white flags to their rifles. Ferguson refused to admit defeat, cut down the white flags, and urged the men to fight on, but his officers realized that to do so would only result in more needless death of their troops. Ferguson tried to ride through the Americans, slashing his sword at anyone who came near, but 8 to 12 Backwoods Riflemen (also known as Overmountain Men) saw Ferguson trying to escape and fired. He was hit numerous times, including one shot to the forehead, knocking him from his saddle. His foot hung in the stirrup and he was dragged over the rocky terrain for a short distance. Seven rifle balls went completely through Ferguson, both of his arms were broken and his clothes were shot to rags. Loyalist Col. Vezey Husbands was also killed in the same volley of fire, Loyalist Col. Ambrose Mills was captured and Maj. Daniel Plummer was seriously wounded. Plummer escaped capture by faking death until it was safe to crawl away. He managed to get to Ninety Six and then to Charleston. This clear American victory exposed Lord Cornwallis' western flank and he immediately retreated from Charlotte, NC to winter camp at Winnsboro, SC. Ferguson was buried at the base of the mountain where he died.

*Marker
The Battle of Kings Mountain Monument

In Memory of the patriotic American who participated in the Battle of Kings Mountain this Monument is erected by their grateful Descendants.

Here the tide of battle turned in favor of the American Colonies.

Here on the 7th day of October A.D. 1780 the British forces commanded by Patrick Ferguson were met and totally defeated by Campbell Shelby, Williams, Cleveland, Sevier, and their heroic followers from Virginia the Carolinas and Tennessee.

Fell on this battle ground in defence of Civil Liberty: Col James Williams. Maj William Chronicle.
—Captains—
John Mattocks. David Beatie. William Edmonson.
—First Lieutenants—
Reece Bowen. Thomas McCullough. William Blackburn. Robert Edmonson
—Second Lieutenants—
John Beatie. Andrew Edmonson. Humberson Lyon. James Corry. James Laird. Nathaniel Guist. Nathaniel Dryden. James Phillips
—Privates—
William Rabb. John Boyd. David Duff. Henry Henigar. William Watson. Arthur Patterson. Preston Goford.

Erected: 1880 by The Kings Mountain Centennial Association.

In Honor of the Three Known African American Patriots
In honor of
the three known African American patriots
and others who participated in the
Battle of Kings Mountain

Esaias Bowman
John Brody
Andrew Ferguson

Marker placed by
The Col. Frederick Hambright Chapter, NSDAR
October 7, 2016

Erected: 2016 by The Col. Frederick Hambright Chapter, NSDAR.

Date visited: _____

Comments: _____

_____

_____

Midlands
Region 1 Site 14

Fort Granby

#1 February 19–21, 1781

#2 May 2–15, 1781

33. 97039°N 81.05012°W

Lexington County

Result: Patriot withdrawal

Combatants	
Loyalist militia	Patriot militia
Commanders and Leaders	
Maj. Andrew Maxwell	Brig. Gen. Thomas Sumter
Strength	
300	280
Casualties and Losses	
unknown	unknown

Fort Granby # 1: February 19–21, 1781: On February 19, 1781, South Carolina militia Brig. Gen. Thomas Sumter, without artillery, laid siege to Fort Granby. Maryland Loyalist Maj. Andrew Maxwell defended this stockade fort with about 300 men. The siege continued for two days while Sumter's men made advances by constructing batteries of logs and tobacco hogsheads as they moved closer to the fort. As news reached Sumter that Lord Rawdon was approaching with a relief column from Camden, the siege was lifted on February 21 and Sumter unexpectedly withdrew down the Congaree.

Result: Patriot victory

Combatants	
Great Britain Loyalist militia	Patriot militia
Commanders and Leaders	
Maj. Andrew Maxwell	Brig. Gen. Thomas Sumter Lt. Col. Henry Lee
Strength	
280 militia and regulars 60 German mercenaries	500
Casualties and Losses	
unknown	unknown

Fort Granby # 2: May 2–15, 1781: On May 2, 1781, with 400 to 500 South Carolina militiamen and State Troops, Gen. Sumter again laid siege to Fort Granby, which was still commanded by Maj. Maxwell. The first was garrisoned by the remnants of the Prince of Wales Regiment and South Carolina Loyalist militia with 340 men. After two days, Sumter took his main force and cannon to move against the British post at Orangeburg, leaving a detachment under South Carolina Patriot militia Col. Thomas Taylor to continue the siege of Fort Granby. After the British surrender of Fort Motte on May 12th, Lt. Col. Henry "Light Horse Harry" Lee arrived at Fort Granby on the evening of May 14 with a six pound cannon and took charge of the siege. Under cover of night and the heavy fog that hung over the fort the next morning, Lee's troops erected a battery within close range of Fort Granby. Maj. Maxwell negotiated the surrender terms and he insisted that the Royal troops should retain all their goods and plunder. Since Lee was afraid that Lord Rawdon might soon arrive from Camden to relieve the fort, Lee agreed to these terms. Sumter's men were infuriated and Sumter himself threatened to resign when he learned the news. Fort Granby surrendered on the morning of May 15, 1781.

Date visited: _____

Comments: _____

_____

Midlands
Region 1 Site 15

Cary's Fort

34. 22100°N 80.63840°W

August 15, 1780

Kershaw County

Result: Patriot victory

Combatants	
Loyalist militia	Patriot militia
Commanders and Leaders	
Maj. Andrew Maxwell Lt. Col. James Cary	Brig. Gen. Thomas Sumter Lt. Col. Henry Lee Col. Thomas Taylor
Casualties and Losses	
7 killed 100 captured	0 killed, wounded, or captured

South Carolina Loyalist militia Lt. Col. James Cary built a fort on his plantation to guard the Wateree Ferry crossing on the west side of the Wateree River. Before the Battle of Camden, Patriot Col. Thomas Sumter, reinforced by Maryland Continentals, a cannon, and North Carolina Patriot militia, deployed to control the Wateree—Catawba River and isolate the British post at Camden. Sumter detached Cols. Thomas Taylor, Edward Lacy and Lt. Col. James Hawthorn to see if Cary's Fort could be taken. The Americans surprised the garrison, killed seven and captured Col. Cary and about 30 Loyalist militia-men. The Patriots also captured 38 wagons of supplies, their teams and 300 head of badly needed cattle.

Sumter learned that a supply and reinforcement convoy was coming from Ninety Six to Camden via the fort. Since Sumter's men looked just like the captured Loyalists, he had no trouble capturing the entire convoy with six wagons of supplies and 70 men from the 71st Highlanders.

Date visited: _____

Comments: _____

_____

_____

Midlands
Region 1 Site 16

Fort Galphin

(Fort Dreadnought)

May 21, 1781

33.31213°N 81.85563°W

Aiken County

Result: Patriot victory

Combatants	
Loyalist militia	Patriot militia
Commanders and Leaders	
Lt. Col. James Cary	Lt. Col. Henry Lee
Capt. Samuel Roworth	Col. Elijah Clarke
Capt. Thomas Hunloke	Col. LeRoy Hammond
	Maj. Allen Mclane
	Lt. Edward Manning
	Col. John Hammond
	Capt. Joseph Wofford
	Maj. Michael Rudolph
Strength	
187	Approx. 2,000
Casualties and Losses	
4 killed	1 killed
unknown wounded	8 wounded
180 captured	0 captured

Lt. Col. Henry Lee commanding his Legion as well as a force of Patriot Militia attacked and captured the fort along with all of its defenders. Lt. Col. Henry Lee was on his way to support GA Col. Elijah Clarke at Beech Island, so he left much of his force and the NC Continentals behind and proceeded to Fort Galphin, where he was joined by a small group of militiamen under Col. LeRoy Hammond. Lt. Col. Lee gave command to Major Michael Rudolph who invested the British post with his infantry, while Lt. Col. Lee's cavalry was sent to cut off any relief from Augusta.

On May 21st, Major Rudolph had the militia make a half-hearted attack on the post and then they slowly moved away, towards the bulk of Major Rudolph's Continentals who were hiding in the pine barrens around the fort. When the defenders sallied out to attack the small militia group, they left the gates open. Major Rudolph rushed in and took possession. The Patriot's only casualty was a man who died from the heat.

Date visited: _____

Comments: _____

_____

_____

Upstate Region

Upstate
Region II

Site #	Location	County	Date
17.	Battle of Cowpens*	Cherokee	January 17, 1781
18.	Battle of Fort Thicketty	Cherokee	July 21, 1780
19.	Battle of Cedar Spring*	Spartanburg	July 12, 1780
20.	Battle of Wofford's Iron Works*	Spartanburg	August 8, 1780
21.	Battle of Blackstock's Plantation*	Union	November 20, 1780
22.	Battle of Musgrove Mill*	Laurens	August 18, 1780
23.	Battle of Great Cane Break*	Greenville	December 22, 1775
24.	Ring Fight*	Oconee	August 12, 1776
25.	Battle of Lyndley's Fort*	Laurens	July 12, 1776
26.	Hammond's Store Action	Laurens	December 30, 1780
27.	Ninety Six #1*	Greenwood	July 17, 1775
	Siege of Ninety Six #2*		November 19–21, 1775
	Siege of Ninety Six #3*		May 21, 1781–
			June 18, 1781
28.	Battle of Long Cane*	McCormick	December 12, 1780

Upstate
Region 2 Site 17

Battle of Cowpens*

January 17, 1781

35.13684°N 81.81837°W

Cherokee County

Result: Patriot victory

Combatants	
Great Britain	United States
	Patriot militia
Commanders and Leaders	
Lt. Col. Banastre Tarleton	Brig Gen. Daniel Morgan
Strength	
1,150	1,065
Casualties and Losses	
110 killed	25 killed
229 wounded	124 wounded
529 captured or missing	

The commanders were the old American wagoneer Brig. Gen. Daniel Morgan and British Lt. Col. Banastre Tarleton. Morgan picked a battleground that put the attacking British in a position with little room to maneuver, since there was a swamp on each side of the road. As the British approached in the early foggy morning, coming up the road to meet Morgan's force, they were unaware of the Americans until it was too late to withdraw.

Morgan's strategy was to put the militia in the front lines, have them fire three volleys and retreat behind the Continental line. This maneuver made Tarleton believe that a rout had started. As the militia retreated and the British charged, the Continentals fired two volleys and retreated in orderly fashion, reloading their muskets with buck and ball as they retreated. In unison, the Continental soldiers turned and fired into the British at a distance of about fifteen feet. The buck and ball at this close range devastated the enemy since it was like being hit with multiple shotguns firing buckshot.

Morgan had hidden his cavalry at the edge of a swamp with a slight rise between them and the British troops. The British cavalry charged past the American lines on their left where they were vulnerable to the American cavalry. The American cavalry charged and decimated the British cavalry. They then attacked the British on their right flank, while the militia regrouped and attacked the British on their left flank.

This action resulted in the defeat of Lt. Col Banastre Tarleton's force, whose remaining men retreated from the battlefield in disarray.

*Marker
Battle of Cowpens Monument

South Inscription:
The Congress of the United States has caused this Monument to be erected on the site of the Battle of Cowpens as a testimonial to the valor and in appreciation of the services of the American Troops on this field in behalf of The Independence of their country.

East Plaque:
British Forces
Lieutenant Colonel Banastre Tarleton Commandant
Tarleton's Legion: 550 men
7th Regiment Maj. Newmarsh: 200 men
1st Battalion of the 71st
Regiment of Maj. McArthur: 200 men
Detachment of the 17th
Regiment of Dragoons: 50 men
Detachment of the Royal
Artillery: 500 men

Total British: 1050 men

North Inscription:
On this field American Troops
under
Brigadier General Daniel Morgan

won a signal victory over a
British Force Commanded by
Lieutenant Colonel Banastre Tarleton
January 17, 1781.

West Plaque:
American Forces
Brigadier General Daniel Morgan, Virginia Commandant
Major Edward Giles, Maryland State Regiment, A.D.C.
Baron de Glasbeech, Volunteer, A.D.C.

Continental Troops
The Light Infantry, Maryland Line,
Continental Establishment
290 men
Lieutenant Colonel John Eager Howard,
Maryland Commandant
Benjamin Brookes, Maryland,
Captain and Brigade Major
Captain Robert Kirkwood, Delaware

Maryland
Capt. Richard Anderson
Capt. Henry Dobson
Lieut. James Ewing
Lieut. Gassaway Watkins
Lieut. Samuel Hanson
Ensign Walter Dyer
Ensign Smith

Virginia
Lieutenant Barnes
Lieutenant Miller
Ensign King

Third Regiment, Light Dragoons
80 men
Lieutenant Colonel William Washington
Virginia, Commandant
Major Richard Gall, Virginia
Captain William Barrett, North Carolina
Lieutenant Henry Bell, Virginia
Cornet James Simons, South Carolina

Lieutenant Thomas Anderson
Maryland, Volunteer

Militia Troops
Colonel Andrew Pickens
South Carolina Commandant
Major James Jackson
Georgia, Brigade Major

Virginia
200 men
Captain Tate
Captain Buchanan
Captain Gilmore
Ensign Combs
Ensign McCorkill
Ensign Wilson

Georgia
100 men
Maj. John Cunningham
Capt. Samuel Hammond
Capt. George Walton
Capt. Joshua Inman

North Carolina
140 men
Maj. Joseph McDowell

South Carolina
115 men
Colonel Thomas Brandon
Colonel John Thomas, Jr.
Colonel Joseph Hays

South Carolina Horsemen
45 men
Colonel James McCall,
Commandant

Total Americans 970 men

Erected: 1932 by United States Congress.

The Battle of Cowpens: Prelude to Victory
On this field on January 17, 1781, Daniel Morgan led his army to a brilliant victory over Banastre Tarleton's force of British regulars. One of only a few successful double envelopments in history, this battle is recognized by historians as one of the most important of the American Revolution.

Erected: by National Park Service.

Morgan's Flying Army
Morgan's army came from many states—the two Carolinas, Delaware, Georgia, Maryland, and Virginia. They were joined by the militia, some of whom had helped destroy the British army of loyalist Americans under Ferguson at Kings Mountain. They camped nearby without tents and nervously awaited the dawn.

Erected: by Cowpens National Battlefield—National Park Service—U.S. Department of the Interior.

Date visited: _____

Comments: _____

_____

_____

**Upstate
Region 2 Site 18**

Battle of Fort Thicketty

34.98551°N 81.71276°W

(Fort Anderson)

July 26, 1780

Cherokee County

Result: Patriot victory

Combatants	
Great Britain Loyalist militia	Patriot militia
Commanders and Leaders	
Capt. Patrick Moore	Col. Isaac Shelby Col. Elijah Clarke Col. Andrew Hampton Maj. Charles Robertson
Strength	
94	600
Casualties and Losses	
94 captured	0 killed and wounded

Fort Thicketty, named after a nearby mountain and creek, was built in 1760 for the Cherokee Indian Wars. Loyalist Capt. Patrick Moore had command of Fort Thicketty, which was situated a quarter of a mile north of Goucher Creek, which empties into Thicketty Creek. American militia Cols. Isaac Shelby, Elijah Clarke, Andrew Hampton, and Maj. Charles Robertson were sent to attack the fort with 600 men, and eliminate the threat from Capt. Moore.

Col. Shelby surrounded the fort on July 26th and demanded that Capt. Moore surrender, but Moore swore to defend the fort to the last man. Shelby then assembled his men in front of the fort so that the Tories could see the size of the opposition. Moore realized that defending the fort would involve a great loss of life to his men, so he surrendered without firing a shot. Moore agreed to surrender the fort on condition that the garrison be paroled, not to serve again during the war unless exchanged; which was agreed willingly by the Americans, as they did not want to be encumbered by prisoners.

The Patriots captured 250 muskets that had been loaded with buck and ball and were standing ready at the gun ports. The muskets loaded in this manner would have been deadly to Shelby's men, who had no cannons with which to breach the fort's log walls.

The British severely censured Capt. Moore for his loss of the fort after the other officers testified that they argued to defend it. It is said, "He pleaded cowardice." Col. Shelby took his spoils of victory to Cherokee Ford on the Broad River, the camp of North Carolina militia Col. Charles Mc-Dowell. This gave the Patriots temporary control of the modern Cherokee County, but the British quickly countered this loss by dispatching Maj. Patrick Ferguson to the area.

Date visited: _____

Comments: _____

_____

_____

Upstate
Region 2 Site 19

Battle of Cedar Spring*
July 12, 1780

34.90931°N 81.87560°W

Spartanburg County

Result: Patriot victory

Combatants	
Loyalist militia	Patriot militia
Commanders and Leaders	
unknown	Col. John Thomas, Jr.
Strength	
150	300
Casualties and Losses	
unknown	0 killed and wounded

In the settlement along upper Fairforest Creek, South Carolina Patriot militia Col. John Thomas, Jr. took command of the Spartan Regiment after the British imprisoned his father at Ninety Six. Mrs. Jane Black Thomas traveled to Ninety Six to visit her husband and while she was there she overheard a Tory mention a plan to surprise her son's regiment the following night at Cedar Springs. She quickly departed Ninety Six and made the 60-mile ride in time to warn Col. Thomas of the intended attack. When the Tories arrived and attacked the camp, they found themselves in an ambush. They rapidly retreated, leaving several dead on the field.

The spring still flows and derived its name from a large cedar tree that once stood on its bank.

*Marker
Battle of Cedar Spring

Not far from this spot on the 8th day of August 1780, was fought the Battle of Cedar Spring, one of a series of engagements in upper South Carolina that made possible the great victory at Kings Mountain and the final success of the American cause at Yorktown.

In grateful commemoration this tablet is erected by the Cowpens Chapter DAR and the Spartanburg Chapter SAR 1928

Erected: 1928 by Cowpens Chapter DAR and the Spartanburg chapter SAR.

Date visited: _____

Comments: _____

_____

_____

**Upstate
Region 2 Site 20**

Battle of Wofford's Iron Works*
(Also known as Second Battle of Cedar Spring)

34.94176°N 81.84532°W

August 8, 1780

Spartanburg County

Result: Patriot victory with a tactical retreat

Combatants	
Great Britain	Patriot militia
Commanders and Leaders	
Maj. James Dunlap	Col. Elijah Clarke
	Col. Isaac Shelby
	Col. William Graham
Strength	
unknown	unknown
Casualties and Losses	
8 killed	4 killed
26 wounded	23 wounded
50 captured	0 captured

To secure the western areas of South Carolina, North Carolina Patriot militia Colonels Isaac Shelby and William Graham and Georgia Point militia Col. Elijah Clarke led an expedition through present day Spartanburg and Union counties. On the morning of August 8, Loyalist Maj. James Dunlop attacked the Patriots at their camp on Fairforest Creek. A fierce battle ensued lasting about ½ hour and involving hand to hand combat between mounted Patriot militia and Tory dragoons. Dunlop's dragoons were finally driven off, but in a few hours Loyalist Maj. Patrick Ferguson's main force arrived.

The Patriots retreated in the direction of Wofford's Iron works on Lawson's Fork Creek, fighting a series of rear guard actions along the way. The Patriot baggage was stored at the Iron Works and a 4 hour long battle raged there until the Patriots withdrew, reaching the secure refuge of a steep hill on the north side of Pacolet River.

*Marker

EARLY IRON WORKS

Near here on Lawson's Fork, during the American Revolution, the S.C. government as part of the war effort supported Joseph Buffington, William Wofford, and others in the construction of an iron works, it became a well-known landmark and the scene of several skirmishes, notably the "Battle of Wofford's Iron Works" on August 8, 1780.

Erected: 1979 by Spartanburg County Historical Association.

Date visited: _____

Comments: _____

_____

_____

**Upstate
Region 2 Site 21**

Battle at Blackstock's Plantation*

34.67917°N 81.81083°W

November 20, 1780

Union County

Result: Patriot victory

Combatants	
Great Britain Loyalist militia	Patriot militia
Commanders and Leaders	
Lt. Col. Banastre Tarleton	Brig. Gen. Thomas Sumter
Strength	
270 regulars and militia	1,000
Casualties and Losses	
8 killed 26 wounded 50 captured	4 killed 23 wounded 0 captured

British Lt. Col. Banastre Tarleton secretly crossed the Broad River to pursue Patriot Brig. Gen. Thomas Sumter. Sumter had gathered over ten militia regiments from Georgia, South Carolina, and North Carolina to attack the British post at Ninety Six. From a defector, Gen. Sumter learned of Tarleton's pursuit, turned his march to the north, and chose to make a stand at Capt. William Blackstock's plantation on the Tyger River. Sumter's men were deployed but cooking when the alarm was given, they quickly took up positions on the high grounds in the house, barn, and along the heavy built fence on the opposite side of a farm lane. Sumter also deployed his troops on top of the hill behind the house and in a wooded area just below the ridge to the west of the house. Sumter, without artillery or trained infantrymen, had placed his riflemen well and chosen the best possible ground to make his stand.

Late in the afternoon, Tarleton's cavalry and mounted infantry raced ahead of his infantry and artillery to "hold Sumter" before the Americans could cross the Tyger River. The British infantry formed at the base of the hill and Sumter sent volunteers forward against the 63rd Regiment infantry to begin the battle. He sent South Carolina militia Col. Edward Lacey's mounted riflemen to circle to the west and get behind the British. Lacey's men were able to get within 75 yards of the British cavalry who were watching the action in the valley below before opening fire. Firing from the high ground and plantation buildings, and being flanked on the east by Sumter's Georgians, the British infantry was penned down in the hollow. To rescue his infantry,

Tarleton's British cavalry charged up the farm lane into the intense rifle fire. As the British charged up the road, dead British and their horses covered the road. Tarleton then ordered a general charge up the farm lane, but he did not know of the Patriots at the fence and in the woods. The British charged up the hill. The 63rd approached the house and outbuilding over an open field. The Patriot fire commenced when the British were 60 yards away and was so heavy from the buildings and the reserves that the 63rd fled in as much confusion as that of the cavalry.

After regrouping his exhausted men, Tarleton retreated to join his straggling infantry and artillery, having lost about half his men in the battle. As darkness came Sumter was badly wounded and was out of action for three months afterward. Sumter relinquished command to Georgia Patriot militia Col. John Twiggs. Twiggs held the field for 2 hours then left campfires burning, forded the Tyger River, and disbanded the militia. Tarleton camped on a hill 2 miles from the battlefield for the night.

Tarleton claimed a victory for dispersing Sumter's militia brigade, but this battle was clearly a costly defeat for the British and a precursor to the action at Cowpens.

*Marker
BATTLE OF BLACKSTOCK'S
This battle of the Revolution took place on William Blackstock's plantation, 3 miles N. on the south side of the Tyger River, November 20, 1780. Gen. Thomas Sumter commanded the American patriots who repulsed Lt. Col. Banastre Tarleton's British forces. Sumter was wounded here, and this prevented his taking an active part in the war for several months.

Date visited: _____

Comments: _____

_____

_____

Upstate
Region 2 Site 22

Battle at Musgrove's Mill*

34.59331°N 81.85276°W

August 18, 1780

Laurens County

Result: Patriot victory

Combatants	
Great Britain	Patriot militia
Commanders and Leaders	
Col. Alexander Innes	Col. Elijah Clarke
Maj. Thomas Fraser	Col. James Williams
Maj. Daniel Clary	Col. Isaac Shelby
Strength	
500	200–300
Casualties and Losses	
63 killed	4 killed
90 wounded	9 wounded
76 captured	

Militia Patriot Colonels, Elijah Clarke of Georgia, Isaac Shelby from western North Carolina, and James Williams of South Carolina, with 200 to 300 mounted militiamen from Georgia, the "Over-Mountain" settlements of North Carolina, and South Carolina, rode from North Carolina militia Col. Charles McDowell's camp at Smith's Ford on the Broad River to attack the Loyalists gathered at Edward Musgrove's Mill on the Enoree River. On the morning of August 19th, some of their men skirmished with an outlying party of the Loyalists at Musgrove Mill. Both sides suffered some wounded, with one Loyalist being killed. The firing alerted British officers Lt. Col. Alexander Innes and Maj. Thomas Fraser who were staying in the Musgrove's residence nearby. The Loyalist militia camped at Musgrove's had been reinforced the previous night with 200 South Carolina Royalist provincial troops under Innes and another 100 provincial troops from New Jersey and New York. South Carolina Loyalist militia Col. Daniel Clary commanded the garrison at the mill. Another 100 Loyalist militia and Maj. Patrick Ferguson with a sizable force were patrolling separately not many miles away. Innes and Fraser decided to attack the rebels immediately, who had moved north up a wooded ridge about two miles from the mill. Except for 100 men to guard his camp, Innes went to attack the Patriots with his remaining troops.

While awaiting the Loyalists' attack, Shelby, Clarke, and William's men built a rough defensive wall in some thirty minutes. Then Capt. Shadrack Inman led a party of 25 men to lure enemy forces into an ambush. The Provincials and Loyalists attempted to take the Patriots with bayonets, but most of their officers, including Innes and Fraser, were wounded at a critical moment. Disorder set in and the British fled.

The Patriots, upon learning of the defeat of the Continental Army under Gen. Gates at Camden, mounted and quickly withdrew. The prisoners were riding double with the Patriots as they avoided the roads and moved as quickly as possible, traveling the 60 miles to reach the safety of Col. Charles McDowell's camp, who had withdrawn back into North Carolina. The important battle demonstrated that American militia could defeat redcoat British regulars, and proved that the multistate cooperation amongst the American militias worked, which provided the American victories at Kings Mountain and Cowpens.

*Marker
Battle of Musgrove Mill

Site of Battle of Musgrove Mill American Revolution August 18, 1780

Date visited: _____

Comments: _____

_____

_____

Upstate
Region 2 Site 23

Battle at Great Cane Brake*

December 22, 1775

34.65576°N 81.31651°W

Greenville County

Result: Patriot victory

Combatants	
Loyalist militia	Patriots militia
Commanders and Leaders	
Capt. Patrick Cunningham	Col. Richard Richardson
	Maj. William "Danger" Thomson
Strength	
500	1,300
Casualties and Losses	
6 killed	1 wounded
unknown wounded	
130 captured	

While those engaged at Ninety Six (after July 14, 1775) were negotiating a truce, Col. Richard Richardson was already on his way into the upcountry to arrest the leaders of the Loyalist party. Col. Richardson decided that his mission was not affected by the truce signed at Ninety Six and proceeded to carry out his instructions.

Receiving intelligence that the most active leaders of the opposition were encamped on Cherokee land, he dispatched a force under Col. William Thomson, which surprised the Loyalists on the morning of December 22 and defeated them in the Battle of Great Cane Brake. Most of the Loyalist band were captured and sent back to face charges of sedition in Charlestown. However, Patrick Cunningham and Col. Joseph Robinson escaped to the Cherokee Nation.

The Great Cane Brake was located on the Reedy River in the southern portion of present Greenville County, The only location Col. Richardson gives us is that the site was a long march of nearly twenty-five miles from his camp at Hollingsworth's Mill on Raborn's Creek (in present-day Laurens County, and the modern spelling is Rabon Creek). Luxuriant growths of cane were quite common in river valleys of the upcountry before the American Revolution.

*Marker
Battle of Great Cane Brake
BATTLE OF GREAT CANE BRAKE
Here along the south side of the Creek to Reedy River was fought. Dec. 22, 1775, The Battle of Great Cane Brake between a force of South Carolinians under Colonel William Thomson and a band of Tories under Patrick Cunningham. The Tories were completely routed. And Cunningham himself narrowly escaped.

Date visited: _____

Comments: _____

_____

_____

Upstate
Region 2 Site 24

Ring Fight*

34.52980°N 83.29100°W

(Tamassee Mountain)

August 12, 1776

Oconee County

Result: Patriot victory

Combatants		
Cherokee warriors		
	Patriot militia	
Commanders and Leaders		
unknown	Capt. Andrew Pickens	
Strength		
185	25	
Casualties and Losses		
65 killed	11 killed	
14 wounded		

A major battle was fought in the vicinity of Tamassee Mountain. Capt. Andrew Pickens and Capt. Robert Anderson were scouting in advance of the main army when they encountered a large party of Native Americans, numbering about 300. Maj. Andrew Williamson's main body soon arrived, and the Cherokee warriors were defeated after a hard-fought battle.

Pickens was leading a scouting party of only 25 men through a field, thick with tall grass, when they were spotted by a force of 185 warriors, who attacked. The warriors encircled them. Pickens and his men maintained calm and fired with speed, accuracy, and timing from their circular formation. The overconfidence on the part of the Cherokees enabled the Patriot militia to throw the warriors into a state of confusion and inflict heavy casualties on them, who outnumbered them greatly. The warriors were already beaten back when Picken's brother, Joseph arrived with reinforcements.

Note: This event is the basis for the legend of the Ring Fight. The ring formation was a standard formation against a force attacking from all sides. As a result, more than one battle is known by this name. This particular Ring Fight was of significance in the career of Andrew Pickens. He considered it the most perilous battle he ever undertook. He later established his last home near the site. According to his grandson, after this battle the indigenous people began to regard Pickens with a kind of awe. Thereafter, they would refer to him by no other name than "Skyagunsta," or Wizard Owl, an expression signifying Great Warrior.

*Marker
RING FIGHT DAR MARKER

Tamassee Town
Near this site once stood the Cherokee "lower town" of Tamassee. On August 12, 1776 a Revolutionary War battle known as the "Ring Fight" was fought here between the Cherokee and the South Carolina Militia under Captain Andrew Pickens. The Cherokee were defeated and many years later Gen. Pickens built his house here when he retired. The Cherokee became his neighbors and friends.

Erected: 2006 by the Oconee Arts and Historical Commission and the Walhalla Chapter of the Daughters of the American Revolution.

Date visited: _____

Comments: _____

_____

_____

Upstate
Region 2 Site 25

Battle at Lyndley's Fort*

July 15, 1776

34.45487°N 82.11581°W

Laurens County

Result: Patriot victory

Combatants	
Loyalist militia Cherokee warriors	Patriot militia
Commanders and Leaders	
Col. David Fanning	Maj. Jonathan Downs
Strength	
190 Loyalists and Cherokee warriors	150
Casualties and Losses	
2 killed 10 captured	unknown

The Cherokee went on the warpath on July 1, 1776. Henry Laurens wrote that the Cherokee attacked "very suddenly, without any pretense to Provocation those treacherous Devils in various Parties headed by White Men", killing as many as 60 South Carolinians. The timing of this campaign was fortuitous for the Cherokee: a major British force had been anchored off Charleston, South Carolina since early June, but its attack on the city had been repulsed in the June 28 Battle of Sullivan's Island. As a result, Continental Army General Charles Lee was unable to provide any sort of relief.

When the Cherokee attacks began in South Carolina, refugees began fleeing the outlying settlements for frontier fortifications. One of these was Lindley's Fort, a vestige of the Anglo-Cherokee War of the early 1760s that was rehabilitated and strengthened by the refugees. A militia company under Major Jonathan Downs arrived at the fort on July 14, raising the total number of armed defenders to about 150.

The next day a force of about 190 Loyalists and Cherokee arrived. Although they attempted an assault on the fort, its stockade walls were sufficient to withstand their weaponry, which was limited to muskets and indigenous weapons such as tomahawks. When the attackers began to abandon the attempt on the fort in favor of easier raiding targets nearby, Major Downs led a sortie from the fort. In a running battle he managed to capture about 10 Loyalists.

*Marker
LYNDLEY'S FORT
On July 15, 1776, a number of Indians and Tories attacked this frontier fort where area settlers had gathered for protection. Major Jonathan Downs, with a company of men, had arrived the previous evening & helped repulse the attack. This victory gave encouragement to the American cause locally. The site is located about 600 yds. South.

Date visited: _____

Comments: _____

_____

_____

Upstate
Region 2 Site 26

Hammond's Store Action

December 30, 1780

34.42570°N 81.87820°W

Laurens County

Result: Patriot victory

Combatants	
Loyalist militia Cherokee warriors	Patriot militia
Commanders and Leaders	
Col. Thomas Waters	Lt. Col. William Washington Maj. James McCall
Strength	
250	280
Casualties and Losses	
150 killed or wounded 40 captured	0 killed wounded, or captured

Only two days after his arrival at Grindal Shoals on the Pacolet River, American Brig. Gen. Daniel Morgan learned that about 250 Georgia Tories, under the command of Georgia Loyalist militia Col. Thomas Waters had advanced to the Fair Forest Creek area, about 20 miles away. These Tories were attacking the homes of Americans from Ninety Six to Winsboro and were also to support Col. Thomas Fletchall's Royal faction there. Morgan dispatched Lt. Col. William Washington to attack them with his 3rd Continental Light Dragoons and 200 of Maj. James McCall's South Carolina State Cavalry. The Tories retreated about 20 miles before Washington could overtake them, but about noon on December 30, the Patriots surprised the enemy camped at Hammond's Old Store just west of the Bush River. The Tories fled their camp and the fight raged around the farm and store buildings. When the fight was over, 150 enemy troops were killed or wounded and 40 were taken prisoner. Due to the one-sided casualties it appears that Waters' troops made no organized stand against Washington and McCall's cavalry.

Waters with 60 men escaped and were chased 7 miles in a running fight south down now SC Highway 56. The chase ended about 3 miles from the Tory occupied Fort Williams, which would have been the destination of the Tories seeking the safety of allies and the fort. At that point, the chase was abandoned and Fort Williams was attacked the next day by the Patriots.

Date visited: _____

Comments: _____

**Upstate
Region 2 Site 27**

Fort Ninety Six*

34.14714°N 82.02341°W

#1 July 17, 1775
#2 November 19–21, 1775
#3 May 21–June 18, 1781

Greenwood County

Result: British victory

Combatants	
Loyalist militia	United States
Commanders and Leaders	
Capt. Moses Kirkland Col. Thomas Fletchall	Lt. Col James Mayson
Strength	
200	unknown
Casualties and Losses	
unknown	unknown

Ninety Six # 1: July 17, 1775: On the question of independence, the sentiment was probably even more divided along the South Carolina coast. Patriot Capt. Moses Kirkland of the South Carolina 3rd Regiment, Col. William Thomson's Rangers, in command of his militia company posted at Ninety Six, changed sides and persuaded his men to abandon the Patriot cause. Kirkland then invited a 200 man Loyalist militia, under Col. Thomas Fletchall, into Ninety Six, giving the Loyalists possession of the town without a fight. Patriot Maj. James Mayson, who had earlier captured the garrison, guns, and military supplies at Fort Charlotte on the Savannah River, was arrested, jailed at Ninety Six, and charged with robbing the King's gunpowder from Fort Charlotte. The Loyalists later released Mayson on bail.

Result: Truce

Combatants	
Loyalist militia	United States
Commanders and Leaders	
Maj. Joseph Robinson	Maj. Andrew Williamson
Strength	
1,900	600
Casualties and Losses	
1 killed	1 killed
52 wounded	12 wounded

Ninety Six # 2: November 19–21, 1775: Patriot Maj. Andrew Williamson and about 600 men built defensive works consisting of wood, hay bales, and beef hides at Savage's Old Field, incorporating barns and outbuildings of Loyalist James Holmes. It was called Williamson's Fort. Loyalist Maj. Joseph Robinson and Capt. Patrick Cunningham with about 1,900 men took over the nearby town, fortified the jail and besieged the Patriots for two days. The siege ended with a truce. This was the Revolution's first land battle south of New England. James Birmingham was the first South Carolina Patriot killed in the Revolution.

The British, after the fall of Charleston in May 1780, quickly moved into the South Carolina backcountry and established regional strategic bases at Camden and Ninety Six. Loyalist militias were organized and the towns were fortified to provide a secure base to administer and control the area. The village of Ninety Six was surrounded by a palisade wall, with fortified block houses; the brick two-story jail was fortified; and two strong detached redoubts were constructed, one on the side of the 1775 Williamson's Fort and another just north of the village, the earthen Star Fort.

Result: British victory

Combatants	
Loyalist militia	United States
Commanders and Leaders	
Lt. Col. John Harris Cruger	Maj. Gen. Nathanael Greene
Capt. Patrick Cuningham	Lt. Col. Henry "Light Horse Harry" Lee
Strength	
550	1,600
Casualties and Losses	
85 killed and wounded	147 killed and wounded

Ninety Six # 3: May 21–June 18, 1781: Patriot Maj. Nathanael Greene with about 1,600 men conducted a classic trench and artillery siege of the fortified garrison of Ninety Six. Loyalist Lt. Col. John Harris Cruger and about 550 Loyalists manned the village and its redoubts. A heavy cannonade caused the British to abandon the Stockade Fort and withdraw into the village, leaving them vulnerable for want of water. Lt. Col. Henry "Light Horse Harry" Lee, returning from his capture of Augusta with prisoners, reinforced Greene. Lee's troops successfully stormed the Stockade Fort and tried against the redoubt built around the jail while Greene attacked the Star Fort. The Loyalists repulsed these assaults on the Star Fort. The approach of British Col. Francis Rawdon with a 2,000-man relief column from Charleston forced Greene to abandon this longest field siege of the war.

*Marker
Ninety Six in the American Revolution
The War in the Southern Colonies

Ninety Six played a significant role in the struggle for American independence from British rule. It was the site of the first southern land battle of the Revolutionary War, in 1775, and the scene of its longest field siege, in 1781. Early in the war the British focused on conquering the North. However, they turned their gaze to the South after suffering setbacks in New York, New Jersey and Philadelphia.

The colonies of Virginia, North Carolina, Georgia, and South Carolina provided cash crops, including rice, indigo and tobacco, to markets in England. Because of this critical economic tie, many southern colonists remained loyal to British rule. They were called "Loyalists." The British Army recruited these Loyalists to help them fight the American revolutionaries called "Patriots," who wanted independence. The battles fought at Ninety Six were between Loyalists and Patriots, all of whom were born on American soil.

The British found that the South was not so easily won. Here in the backcountry of South Carolina residents changed alliances frequently — siding with the Loyalists when it seemed to their advantage but supporting the Patriots when they felt oppressed by British rule. At Ninety Six the town was firmly in the hands of the Patriots in 1775, but became Loyalist territory by 1780, just before the siege of Ninety Six took place on these grounds.

Emerging victorious in the southern battles of Kings Mountain and Cowpens, the Patriots held their ground and pushed the British northward, forcing their surrender at Yorktown in October, 1781. But the war did not end immediately. Bloody battles of revenge between Patriots and Loyalists consumed areas of South Carolina, until a final peace treaty was signed between the United States and Britain in 1783.

Erected: by National Park Service: Ninety Six National Historical Site.

Why Is It Called Ninety Six?
A Colonial Backcountry Settlement

The origin of Ninety Six's unusual numeric name remains a mystery. There are many theories. One plausible explanation is that English traders who passed through here in the 1700s estimated this location to be 96 miles from the Cherokee village of Keowee to the northwest, near present-day Clemson. The first known historical reference to Ninety Six is on a map of 1730, created by George Hunter, surveyor general of South Carolina.

Long before the Europeans arrived in the 1700s—as early as 900 B.C.—bands of hunter-gatherers roamed here. The heavily forested land changed with time, as did the native groups, who began to clear fields for farming, weave cloth from natural fibers, and fashion pottery from the area's red clay soil. Of the many Indian groups who inhabited the backcountry near Ninety Six, it was the Cherokee who predominated and used this area as their hunting grounds.

Positioned at the crossroads of several critical trade routes that linked Cherokee territory to the city of Charleston on the coast, Ninety Six became a seat of power in the British colony of South Carolina. The town offered settlers a safe haven, fertile fields, and ample wildlife. Captain George Chicken of the colonial militia recorded that he "killed a boflow" when camping here with his men in 1716.

Steady population growth around Ninety Six eventually led to hostilities between European settlers and Indians. A fort built on this site withstood Indian attacks in 1760.

Erected: 2009 by National Park Service.

The Siege of Ninety Six
1781

In November 1775 — just months after American and British troops traded musket fire at Lexington and Concord, Massachusetts — the first southern land battle of the Revolutionary War was fought here in Ninety Six. Later, in 1781, the longest field siege of that war — 28 days — took place at Ninety Six. After an unsuccessful final assault by the Patriots, American forces withdrew. One month later, the British abandoned Ninety Six, laying the fort and town to ruin.

The site of the siege of 1781 offers a unique opportunity to see Revolutionary War earthworks and understand how warfare was waged in the 1700s. The story of the siege also offers insight into the strategies used by commanders of the opposing armies: Lieutenant Colonel John Harris Cruger of the British Army and Major General Nathanael Greene of the American Continental Army.

Erected: 2009 by National Park Service.

Ninety Six National Historic Site
A Revolutionary War Landmark

Ninety Six National Historic Site is a unit of the National Park Service, which preserves lands of national significance. This park features the site of the old town of Ninety Six, an important seat of power in the backcountry of South Carolina during colonial times. The park includes some of the best preserved earthworks—the Star Fort and a military mine—of the American Revolution. Here you can follow the trails of the Cherokee Indians who first hunted these woods, explore the land where early traders, colonists, and African slaves settled, and visit the scene of struggles for independence from Britain during the Revolutionary War.

Erected: 2009 by National Park Service.

Date visited: _____

Comments: _____

_____

_____

Upstate
Region 2 Site 28

Battle of Long Cane*
December 12, 1780

34.03198°N 82.39416°W

McCormick County

Result: British victory (Patriots had to retreat)

Combatants		
Great Britain		United States
Loyalist militia		Patriot militia
Commanders and Leaders		
Lt. Col. Isaac Allen		Col. Elijah Clarke
		Col. Benjamin Few
Strength		
450		100
Casualties and Losses		
2 killed		14 killed
9 wounded		7 wounded
0 captured		9 captured

After Col. Elijah Clarke had brought many of the Patriot families of upper Georgia to the sanctuary of the Watauga settlements, he and his men (a number of whom were at Kings Mountain and Blackstocks) returned to Georgia. Sometime in December he was again in the field and with Col. Benjamin Few. (Few having seniority over Clarke.) With their combined force, they advanced on the Long Cane Creek settlement just southwest of Ninety Six. Upon their arrival at Long Cane they sought to enlist recruits from the settlement which had a strong Patriot leaning.

Brig. Gen. Robert Cunningham, the Loyalist commander in the area, sent a request to Lt. Col. John Cruger at Ninety Six for support. Lt. Col. Cruger dispatched 200 New Jersey Volunteers, 200 Loyalist militia, and 50 dragoons. Initially, the Loyalists were forced to retreat in the face of the attack by Patriots. Thinking their enemy to be only militia, Patriots attacked the British camp and intended to fight a delaying action until the main body of Americans could be brought up. Col.

Clarke, who was wounded, then called on Col. Benjamin Few to support him, but Col. Few was unable to do so, nor tell Col. Clarke he had decided to withdraw. As a result, Col. Clarke and the Patriots were driven back. The British regulars formed and attacked with bayonets. The Americans were routed by the British regular troops. The Loyalists then chased the Americans during their retreat. Col. Clarke's wound, which was at first thought mortal, kept him from further fighting till early March, 1781.

The Battle of Long Cane was a running battle covering 4.6 to 6 miles in a big arc from its beginning 2.5 miles west of the British camp, east to the British camp, then the British pushed back through Col. Elijah Clark's camp, to its end at Col. Benjamin Few's camp.

*Marker
Battle of Long Cane
About four miles southeast is the site of the American Revolutionary Battle of Long Cane. On December 12, 1780, Lieutenant Colonel Isaac Allen and a British force of 400–500 men defeated Colonel Elijah Clarke and 100 Americans, an advanced detachment of a Patriot force commanded by Colonel Benjamin Few.

Erected: 1977 by McCormick County Historical Commission.

Date visited: _____

Comments: _____

_____

_____

Pee Dee Region

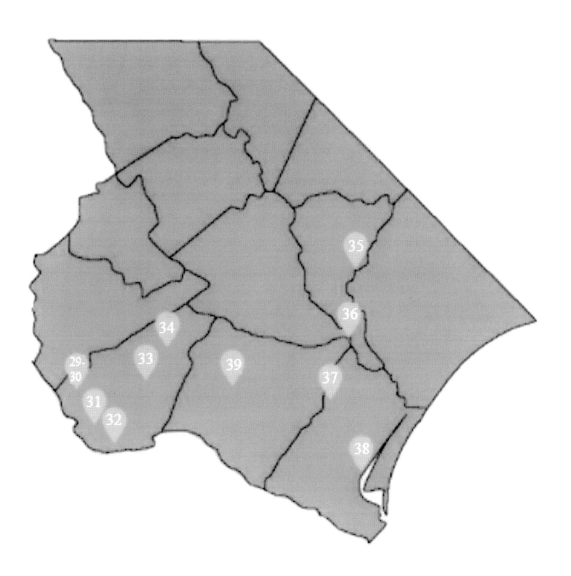

Pee Dee
Region III

Site #	Location	County	Date
29.	High Hills of Santee* (Thomas Sumter's Gravesite)	Sumter	May 27, 1780
30.	Battle of Halfway Swamp*	Clarendon	December 12–13, 1780
31.	Siege of Fort Watson*	Clarendon	April 15–23, 1781
32.	Battle of Great Savannah	Clarendon	August 25, 1780
33.	Battle of Ox Swamp*	Clarendon	November 8, 1780
34.	Battle of Tearcoat Swamp*	Clarendon	October 25, 1780
35.	Battle of Blue Savannah*	Marion	August 4, 1780
36.	Snow's Island*	Florence	March 23, 1781
37.	Battle of Black Mingo*	Williamsburg	September 14, 1780
38.	Occupation of Georgetown*	Georgetown	July 1, 1780– January 24, 1781
39.	Battle of Kingstree*	Williamsburg	September 6, 1780

**Pee Dee
Region 3 Site 29**

High Hills of Santee*
(Gravesite of Thomas Sumter)
May 27, 1780

33.98699°N 80.51737°W

Sumter County

British Lt. Col. Banastre Tarleton was detached from Lord Cornwallis' army to chase Col. Abraham Buford's Virginia Continentals after the fall of Charlestown. Tarleton detached Capt. Charles Campbell to burn Col. Thomas Sumter's home. This act enraged Sumter and reactivated the retired Continental officer as South Carolina's Patriot militia leader. Tories burned Col. Sumter's house. It was later rebuilt and thereafter known as "The Ruins." Gen. Sumter owned 10,000 acres in this area, including Edgehill Plantation which he used as a Headquarters when in the area.

*Marker
Thomas Sumter
Symbol of South Carolina Resistance

"Enchanted with the splendor of victory, he (Thomas Sumter) would wade in torrents of blood to attain it. "
Colonel Henry "Light Horse Harry" Lee.

The land on which you now stand, here in the High Hills of Santee, once belonged to General Thomas Sumter. Today, only the graves of Sumter and many of his descendants remain as a vestige of his residence. Most of his exploits during the American Revolutionary War (1775–1783), Sumter contributed greatly to the ultimate defeat of British forces in South Carolina. Sumter distinguished himself most notably in 1780, after the British captured Charleston and then marched into the Carolina backcountry. Many patriots, disheartened by a series of British victories, laid down their weapons—but not Thomas Sumter. Earning the nickname "The Fighting Gamecock," he organized a partisan band of guerilla fighters who so harassed the King's troops that British General Lord Cornwallis considered Sumter his "greatest Plague." Sumter, who preferred the freedom of independent command, sometimes disregarded the orders of his superiors and clashed with fellow officers. Nevertheless, the "Gamecock" kept the spirit of Revolution alive in South Carolina at a critical time.

Having outlived every other Revolutionary War general, he died in 1832, at a remarkable age of 98. In 1907, the South Carolina General Assembly honored Sumter's service and sacrifice by erecting the granite monument that stands in the cemetery before you.

Map Included: South Carolina:
Between July 1780 and July 1781 General Sumter struggled with British Forces in six important engagements, keeping the cause of independence alive after the fall of
Charleston.

Born on the Virginia frontier in 1734, Sumter's military career spanned the French and Indian War (1756–1763) and the American Revolution. Plagued by financial troubles in Virginia, Sumter came to South Carolina in 1763 in search of new economic opportunity. He opened a store near Nelson's Ferry, on the Santee River, and went on to become one of the most prominent merchants and planters in the backcountry.

Erected: by General Sumter Memorial Park.

Date visited: _____

Comments: _____
_____
_____

Pee Dee
Region 3 Site 30

Battle of Halfway Swamp*

33.65601°N 80.49650°W

December 12–13, 1780

Clarendon County

Result: Patriot victory

Combatants	
Great Britain	Patriot militia
Commanders and Leaders	
Maj. Robert McLeroth	Col. Francis Marion
Strength	
300–500	300–500
Casualties and Losses	
333	10–12 killed or wounded

British Maj. Robert McLeroth with the 64th Regiment was escorting 200 recruits of the 7th Regiment Fusiliers to Camden from Charleston. American Col. Francis Marion learned of his march and set out to overtake him. Marion caught McLeroth near Halfway Swamp and drove McLeroth's men into an open field north of the swamp. Marion engaged McCottry's riflemen and killed several British pickets. McLeroth's envoy, under a flag of truce, argued that shooting pickets was uncivilized warfare. He proposed that 20 of Marion's men do battle with 20 British regulars the next day to save many casualties on both sides. These 40 men would determine the winner. That engagement would substitute for an all out fight between all the men of the American and British forces. Marion chose Maj. John Vanderhorst to command the best American riflemen for the action. The next day, when Vanderhorst marched within 100 yards of the 20 British regulars armed with muskets and bayonets, the British shouldered their arms and retreated. Vanderhorst and Marion had been tricked, since the British had built large bonfires that night to again fool the Americans. With the fires blazing, the British slipped away during the night leaving their baggage behind. The British marched north on the Old River Road toward Singleton's Mill.

*Marker
Halfway Swamp:
"… In pursuit of a Brother to Kill Him"

In December 1781, Maj. Robert McLeroth and the 64th Regiment were conducting newly-arrived British army recruits of the Royal Fusiliers from Charleston to the High Hills of Santee. Learning of McLeroth's movement, Col. Francis Marion led some 700 militiamen up the Santee River Road and surprised McLeroth near Halfway Swamp. McLeroth bought time to avoid a battle by proposing a staged combat, twenty men on each side, and then withdrawing his troops north toward Singleton's Mill during the night.

When Marion discovered McLeroth's trick the next morning, he sent horsemen under Maj. John James in pursuit. Just beating the British to Singleton's Mill ~ a large rice plantation and grist mill located ten miles north ~ James's men seized the buildings and managed to deliver one volley before they realized that the Singletons were ill with smallpox. As quickly as they had come, the Whigs abandoned the plantation to the British. The next day Marion moved his men back down the Santee Road.

British commanders in South Carolina were dissatisfied with McLeroth's performance in the field, but several Patriot sources attest to his uprightness and generosity. After the skirmishing between Halfway Swamp and Singleton's Mill, McLeroth took the wounded from both sides to a tavern, paid for two weeks' lodging, and left an army physician to care for them. When Marion discovered what McLeroth had done, he said to one of his officers: "Well, I suppose I feel now very much as I would feel were I in pursuit of a brother to kill him."

Erected 2012 by Francis Marion Trail Commission of Francis Marion University.

Date visited: _____

Comments: _____

_____

_____

Pee Dee
Region 3 Site 31

Battle of Fort Watson*

33.53906°N 80.43662°W

#1 February 27, 1781

#2 March 1, 1781

#3 April 15–23, 1781

Clarendon County

Result: British victory

Combatants	
Great Britain Loyalist militia	Patriot militia
Commanders and Leaders	
Lt. Col. James Mackay	Brig. Gen. Thomas Sumter Gen. Francis Marion Lt. Col. Henry "Light Horse Harry" Lee
Strength	
Reinforced with 400	unknown
Casualties and Losses	
115 killed or captured	18 killed and many wounded

Battle of Fort Watson #1: Captured Baggage Action: February 27, 1781: After American Brig. Gen. Thomas Sumter captured the British baggage train at Big Savannah, he sent the captured baggage and supplies down the Santee River. The British troops from Fort Watson captured Sumter's boats carrying the baggage and supplies. All the supplies recaptured by the British and needed by Sumter were stored at Fort Watson.

Result: British victory

Combatants	
Great Britain Loyalist militia	Patriot militia
Commanders and Leaders	
Ens. Richard Cooper Maj. John Harrison	Brig. Gen. Thomas Sumter
Strength	
20	200
Casualties and Losses	
unknown	18 killed Many wounded

Battle of Fort Watson #2: Sumter's Wagon Guard Attack 2: March 1, 1781: Sumter needed the supplies recaptured by the British, so he decided to attack Fort Watson. At noon on March 1, 1781, he attacked British Ensign Richard Cooper and 20 men of the Provincial Light Infantry who had fallen behind the rest of the detachment due to a broken wagon axle. Sumter's 200 men surrounded Ens. Cooper's men and demanded that they surrender. Cooper replied that the Light Infantry never surrendered and held off Sumter's men in an intense fight until Loyalist Maj. John Harrison's provincial cavalry corps arrived from Fort Watson, made a charge, and drove Sumter's men away.

Battle of Fort Watson #2: Sumter's Attack on Fort Watson 2: March 1, 1781: Sumter's attack on Fort Watson, (same day—March 1, 1781) was met with intense fire that drove his troops back with 18 killed, many wounded, including Lt. Col. James Hawthorne, and 40 horses captured. A second assault of the Fort was not tried. Sumter withdrew to the Black River. (Fort Watson had been erected in 1780 by and named for British Lt. Col. John Watson Tadwell-Watson, of the Provincial Light Infantry regiment.)

Result: Patriot victory

Combatants	
Great Britain	Patriot militia
Commanders and Leaders	
Lt. James Mackay	Gen. Francis Marion
	Lt. Col. Henry Lee
	Lt. Col. Hezekiah Maham
Strength	
114	400
Casualties and Losses	
144 surrendered	2

Battle of Fort Watson #3: Marion's Attack on Fort Watson: April 15–23, 1781: Gen. Francis Marion and Lt. Col. Henry Lee began their campaign against the British Santee River posts when Lee joined Marion on April 14th. The following day the two commanders marched to Fort Watson, the British post situated on an indigenous mound near Scott's Lake. The American forces laid siege to Fort Watson on the afternoon of April 15 and posted troops to cut off the British access to Scott's Lake, which deprived the British of their only water supply. British Lt. James Mackay countered this move by sinking a well within the British defensive line. American Lt. Col. Hezekiah Maham erected a wooden tower to cover their ground approach and allowed the Americans to shoot down into the British fort on top of the indigenous mound; this tower was completed on the morning of April 23. Under cover of rifle fire from the tower, American troops secured a foothold on the side of the mound and began demolishing the fort's abatis and palisade wall. Fearful that the attackers would mine his position and that he would be unable to force his mutinous troops to defend the post any longer, Mackay surrendered Fort Watson. Marion and Lee had destroyed a vital link in a British supply line from Charleston to Camden.

*Marker
Siege of Fort Watson

During the American Revolution, Colonel Lee and his Legion joined General Marion's Brigade along the Santee River. They laid seige to British held Fort Watson on top of Santee Indian Mound. Major Maham's idea was to build a tower for sharpshooters to fire inside the fort. After days of chopping saplings, they erected the tower overnight. April 23,1781 at dawn, firing from the tower led to rapid surrender of Fort Watson.

Erected: 2009 by Citizens of Clarendon County, SC Public Service Authority (Santee Cooper), Clarendon County Chamber of Commerce.

Date visited: _____

Comments: _____

_____

_____

Pee Dee
Region 3 Site 32

Great Savannah

(Nelson's Ferry)

August 25, 1780

33.48590°N 80.34482°W

Clarendon County

Result: Patriot victory

Combatants	
Great Britain Loyalist militia	Patriot militia
Commanders and Leaders	
Capt. Jonathan Roberts	Col. Francis Marion Maj. Hugh Horry
Strength	
unknown	unknown
Casualties and Losses	
24 killed & wounded	2 wounded

The British captured many American Continental prisoners at Camden. They were taken down the Charleston road to Charleston in groups of 150. On the way, one group of 150 American prisoners were being held at Col. Thomas Sumter's plantation home near the northern edge of the Great Savannah north of Nelson's Ferry. To rescue the American prisoners, Col. Francis Marion ordered the ferry road crossing at Horse Creek seized by himself with 16 of his men and Maj. Hugh Horry with his men. Horry's men stumbled across a sentry at the plantation, who fired a shot. Immediately, Horry attacked the front of the house, with Marion's men attacking the back. Horry discovered the British muskets stacked outside the front door, putting the British at a distinct disadvantage. After a brief skirmish, the Americans killed or took 22 British regulars and 2 Loyalist guides prisoner. Marion released 147 of the Camden prisoners from the Maryland and Delaware Continental Line. However, 85 of those released refused to join Marion's men and asked to continue to Charleston as British prisoners.

Date visited: _____

Comments: _____

_____

_____

**Pee Dee
Region 3 Site 33**

Battle at Ox Swamp*

November 8, 1780

33.42941°N 80.11875°W

Clarendon County

Result: Patriot victory

Combatants	
Great Britain	Patriot militia

Commanders and Leaders	
Lt. Col. Banastre Tarleton	Col. Francis Marion

Strength	
unknown	Approx 400

Casualties and Losses	
0	0

As soon as Lt. Col. Banastre Tarleton received intelligence of Col. Francis Marion's position and had a guide, he commenced his rapid march to Marion's camp near Gen. Richard Richardson's home on the Santee River, which Tarleton contemplated as another scene of slaughter; but Marion had already departed. Tarleton pursued Marion to the Woodyard Swamp but could not pass it at night. The next morning, Marion, knowing his foe, decamped and traveled to Black River for 35 miles, through woods, swamps, and bogs, where there were no roads. He camped the following night on advantageous ground at Benbow's Ferry about ten miles above Kingstree on the east side of Black River. His position was the best defensible ground around. His first defense was the Black River itself and after that at each of three difficult to cross swamps all within ten miles on the east side of the river before he reached Kingstree. On the road to the west was at the river, here, Marion determined to make a stand and felled trees across the road to impede the British.

On the morning after Marion's retreat, Tarleton found Marion's trail across the Woodyard Swamp but went around it and pursued, as he says, "for seven hours, through swamps and defiles." In fact, he pursued about 25 miles, when arriving at Ox Swamp, which was wide, miry, and with no road to pass it. Here, Tarleton abandoned the pursuit of Marion, saying to his men, "Come my boys! Let us go back, and we will soon find the Gamecock [Gen. Sumter], but as for this damned old fox, the devil himself could not catch him." Tarleton had been recalled by his commander, Lord Cornwallis, as SC Patriot militia Brig. Gen. Thomas Sumter was then perceived by Lord Cornwallis as the greater threat.

*Marker

During the American Revolution, on Nov. 8, 1780, General Francis Marion and his brigade lured British Colonel Tarleton and his Green Dragoons about 26 miles from Jack's Creek through the swamps to Ox Swamp, less than 1 mile east of here. After spending six hours in this pursuit, Tarleton gave up the chase saying "…as for the old fox (Marion), the devil himself could not catch him." Thus, General Marion became known as the "Swamp Fox".

Erected: 2001 by the citizens of Clarendon County, Manning and the Clarendon County Chamber of Commerce.

Ox Swamp
The Swamp Fox Earns His Name

On the night of November 7, 1780, Lt. Colonel Banastre Tarleton and his Green Dragoons—together with Harrison's Provincials, a large unit of Tories from the area between the upper Santee and Wateree Rivers—camped at the plantation of the late General Richard Richardson, hoping to surprise Francis Marion's much smaller force.

Marion learned the size of Tarleton's force and in the dead of night withdrew east over Jack's Creek toward the Pocotaligo River and Kingstree. Just before dawn Tarleton received word of Marion's move and by daybreak was in full pursuit, galloping twenty-six miles "through Swamps, Woods, and Fastness toward Black River without a Halt." But when they arrived at the wide, roadless expanse of Ox Swamp, they stopped, exhausted. Tarleton reportedly said to his troops, "Come my boys! Let us go back, and we will soon find the Gamecock (General Thomas Sumter, another Patriot partisan leader). But as for this damned old fox, the devil himself could not catch him." The story spread until all the people along the Santee and the Pee Dee called Francis Marion the "Swamp Fox."

Marion had an ambuscade set for Tarleton at Benbow's Ferry ten miles east of Ox Swamp on the Black River.

Unable to catch Marion, Tarleton punished the surrounding community. Marion reported: "Col. Tarleton has burnt all the houses, and destroyed all the corn, from Camden down to Nelson's Ferry... It is distressing to see women and children sitting in the open air around a fire, without a blanket, or any clothing but what they had on..., for he spares neither Whig nor Tory."

Erected: 2012 by Francis Marion Trail Commission.

Date visited: _____

Comments: _____

_____

_____

Pee Dee
Region 3 Site 34

Battle of Tearcoat Swamp*
October 25, 1780

33.81166°N 80.14194°W

Clarendon County

Result: Patriot victory

Combatants	
Great Britain	Patriot militia
Commanders and Leaders	
Lt. Col. Samuel Tynes	Col. Francis Marion
Strength	
80	150
Casualties and Losses	
6 killed 14 wounded 23 captured	3–26 killed or wounded

Lt. Col. Samuel Tynes, operating in the vicinity of the High Hills area between Salem and Nelson's Ferry, had been able to call up about 200 men whom he armed with stores coming from Camden.

When Col. Francis Marion, at Britton's Neck, learned of Lt. Col. Tynes encampment he was able to call together 150 men (or up to 400 according to one source). Col. Marion crossed the Pee Dee at Port's Ferry, then crossed Lynches Creek (now named Lynches River) at Witherspoon's Ferry and thus made his way to Kingstree. From there he tracked Lt. Col. Tynes to Tearcoat Swamp "in the fork of Black river," where he surprised the Loyalists.

Lt. Col. Tynes and his men were scattered, and a few days later Lt. Col. Tynes and a few of his officers were captured by a detachment of Col. Marion's commanded by Capt. William Clay Snipes. Lt. Col. Tynes lost 6 killed, 14 wounded, and 23 taken prisoner. As well, he lost 80 horses and saddles and as many muskets. Lt. Col. Tynes himself and a few of his officers were captured in the couple of days following the action, though they subsequently escaped.

Col. Marion's own losses were anywhere from 3–26 killed and wounded. Many of Lt. Col. Tynes' men actually came in and enlisted with Col. Marion, who sent his prisoners to North Carolina Brigadier General Henry William Harrington at Cheraw, and proceeded to set up his camp at Snow Island for the <u>first time</u>.

Following Lt. Col. Tynes' defeat, Lt. General Charles, Lord Cornwallis had 50 men sent from Charlestown to Moncks Corner, while maintaining patrols covering his line of communication along the Santee River.

*Marker
Battle of Tearcoat

During the American Revolution, a few miles south of Turbeville, General Marion and his militia routed the British. General Marion learned Colonel Tynes with over ninety troops was camped at the edge of Tearcoat Swamp. On Oct. 25, 1780, Marion moved swiftly toward Tearcoat and attacked at midnight. Marion's Patriots captured food, muskets, and horses.

Erected: 2002 by The citizens of Clarendon County and the Town of Turbeville and the Chamber of Commerce.

Date visited: _____

Comments: _____
_____
_____

Pee Dee
Region 3 Site 35

Battle of Blue Savannah*

34.06991°N 79.30709° W

September 4, 1780

Marion County

Result: Patriot victory

Combatants	
Loyalist Militia	Patriot militia
Commanders and Leaders	
Maj. Micajah Ganey	Lt. Col. Francis Marion
Strength	
200	52
Casualties and Losses	
30 killed and wounded	4 wounded

Excerpt of a letter from Lt. Col. Francis Marion to Maj. Gen. Horatio Gates dated September 15th, 1780, "On the 3rd Instant [September, 1780] I had advice, that upwards of 200 Torys intended to attack me the next day. I immediately marched with 52 men, which is all I could get, on the 4th in the morning I surprised a party of 45 men which I mistook for the main body. I killed and wounded all but 15 which escaped. I then marched immediately to attack the main body, which I met about 3 miles [at Blue Savannah] in full march towards me. I directly attacked them and put to flight (though they had 200 men) and got into an impassable swamp Back Swamp] to all but Torys. I had one man wounded in the first Action and 3 in the second and two horses killed; finding it impossible to come at them I retreated to Camp—the next day I was informed they all disperst—On the 5th I was joined by about 60 men; I then threw up a small redoubt to secure my Camp from being surprised by the Tories Should they again collect."

SC Loyalist militia Maj. Micajah Ganey's advanced guard was the 1st action as Marion moved north along SC Hwy 41 from his base at Port's Ferry. Local residents of the Savannah during the Revolution, named Lewis and Wall, were among the Tories gathered at Blue Savannah and were probably included in Ganey's advanced guard. Blue Savannah was the 2nd action as stated in Marion's letter, noting the impenetrability of the swamp, written about 11 days after the action.

Note: Blue Savannah is a Carolina Bay. Blue Savannah was named for the blue water in the savannah (bay), which was sometimes knee deep, and the blue mud that stuck to wagon wheels crossing the savannah. Both had a bluish color. "Carolina Bay" is a regional term for a geographical feature, probably a depression caused by a meteor strike thousands of years ago, which over time filled with water to create what the early settlers called "bays." There are several of these scattered all across South Carolina. The Blue Savannah bay is now a faint oval image and the sand rim can be seen as a change in color of the soil. Carolina Bays are oval depressions in the land oriented southeast to northwest, each one surrounded by a sandy rim, often filled with water.

*Marker
Battle of Blue Savannah

One fourth mile south of this site General Francis Marion defeated a band of Tories under Captain Barfield on August 13, 1780, by feigning retreat and drawing them into a trap.

Erected: 1955 by Blue Savannah Chapter, Daughters of the American Revolution, Mullins, South Carolina.

Date visited: _____

Comments: _____

_____

_____

Pee Dee
Region 3 Site 36

Snow's Island*

33.84250°N 79.34111°W

March 23, 1781

Florence County

Result: British victory

Combatants	
Great Britain	Patriot militia
Commanders and Leaders	
Lt. Col. Welbore Ellis Doyle	Col. Hugh Ervin
Strength	
300	50
Casualties and Losses	
0	7 killed
	15 captured

South Carolina Patriot Brig. Gen. Francis Marion established a camp on the Great Pee Dee River at a site ideally suited for defense. Snow's Island was a fairly large area of river swamp with some highlands, protected on all sides by water. It is bounded on the north by Lynches Creek, on the east by the Pee Dee River, and on the west by Muddy Creek. Marion's camp was on the northern part of the island, which was the property owned by William Goddard. The island is the southeast corner of Florence County and was named for Goddard's uncles, James and William Snow. Despite several archaeological investigations, the exact location of Marion's base camp on Snow's Island has not been discovered. Most of Snow's Island is periodically flooded.

While Marion was occupied fighting British Col. John Watson at Wyboo Swamp, Mount Hope Swamp and the Lower Bridge south of Kingstree, Col. Welbore Ellis Doyle made his way to Marion's base at Snow's Island. South Carolina Patriot militia Col. Hugh Ervin was in command in Marion's absence. He had the stores of arms and ammunition destroyed to prevent them from falling into the hands of the British. A short bloody skirmish was fought, but the superior British force crossed to the island and completed the destruction of Marion's base.

*Marker

Marion's Camp at Snow's Island

During the American Revolution Gen. Francis Marion (ca. 1732–1795), the most successful of the Patriot partisan leaders, made his camp and headquarters about 1.8 mi. SSW on Snow's Island. The island, named for settlers James and William Snow, is bounded by the Pee Dee River, Lynche's River, and Clark's Creek.

Reverse

Marion, called "the Swamp Fox," led a S.C. militia brigade that camped on the island in the winter of 1780 – 81. In March 1781, with Marion and his men absent, Loyalist under Col. Welborn Doyle raided and destroyed the camp. Marion continued to frustrate British and Loyalist commanders until the end of the war.

Erected: 2012 by The Blue Savannah—Swamp Fox Chapter, Daughters of the American Revolution.

Date visited: _____

Comments: _____

_____

_____

Pee Dee
Region 3 Site 37

Battle of Black Mingo*

3.62234°N 79.43300°W

September 14, 1780

Williamsburg County

Result: Patriot victory

Combatants	
Loyalist militia	Patriot militia
Commanders and Leaders	
Col. John Coming Ball	Col. Francis Marion
Strength	
46	350
Casualties and Losses	
3 killed	2 killed
1 wounded	8 wounded
13 captured	

South Carolina militia Col. Francis Marion was informed that a party of Tories, more numerous than his own party, lay at Black Mingo Creek under the command of South Carolina Loyalist militia Col. John Coming Ball. Ball might soon be reinforced so Marion decided to attack him. The Tories were posted at Shepherd's ferry, on the south one mile above the ferry over a boggy navigable tidal creek, and commanded the passage. Col. Marion had to cross the creek one mile above the ferry over a boggy causeway and bridge of planks. It was almost midnight when his force arrived at the bridge and while the party was crossing, an alarm gun was heard in the Tory camp. The colonel immediately ordered his men to follow him in full gallop. Close to Dollard's "Red House" tavern, they dismounted, excpt a small body which acted as cavalry. Marion ordered a corps of supernumerary officers under the command of Capt. Thomas Waties to proceed down the road and attack Dollard's, where he believed the Tories to be. At the same time, he detached two companies to the right under Col. Hugh Horry and the cavalry to the left to support the attack. Before the corps of officers could reach the house, the men on the right had encountered the enemy, who had left the house and were in a field opposite. This circumstance removed the element of surprise for the Patriots, and at the great urgings of Capt. John James, and the Tories, being attacked on their flank by the corps of officers, and finding themselves between two fires, gave way after a few rounds and took refuge in Black Mingo swamp, which was in their rear. This action was of short duration and was so closely and sharply contested. Marion captured Ball's prized horse, which he named "Old Ball" and rode throughout his partisan campaigns.

Note: It must be remembered that this action took place about midnight. Because of the night's silence, the horses' hooves could be heard on the wood bridge planks. Marion followed Black Mingo Creek to the skirmish site while the officers proceeded down Willtown Road to Black Mingo Church Road and took it east before turning on the road north to attack the British from the south. Caught in the crossfire, the British fled into the swamp.

*Marker
SKIRMISH AT BLACK MINGO CREEK
On Sept. 14, 1780, Gen. Francis Marion's Patriots routed a Tory force commanded by Capt. Thomas Waties and the other by Col. Peter Horry fled into Black Mingo Swamp. The short but sharply-contested action cost each side nearly one-third of its men.

Erected: 2005 by Georgetown County Historical Society, replacing a marker erected by Georgetown County in 1941.

Black Mingo Creek:
Fighting Among Neighbors

In September 1780, Francis Marion returned to South Carolina after a short tactical retreat into the swamps of eastern North Carolina. Hearing that British and Loyalist forces were burning the homes of Whig militiamen in Williamsburg District, Col. Marion aimed to challenge their control of the area.

Marion marched his men across the Great Pee Dee and Lynches Rivers to strike at a Tory detachment at Sheppard's Ferry on Black Mingo Creek. Stationed at Patrick Dollard's tavern less than a mile downstream from the trading village of Willtown, some fifty Tory militiamen under the command of Capt. John Coming Ball guarded the ferry crossing.

Arriving at night, Marion crossed the Black Mingo on a bridge at Willtown. The sound of the horses' hooves on the wooden planks roused the Tories, who formed a line in a clearing

opposite Dollard's tavern (located across the creek from you on the other side of the bridge). Marion divided his force into three detachments, attempting to surround them. The brief but bloody fight sent most of the Tories fleeing into the nearby swamps (behind you on this side of the creek), leaving the Whigs with a considerable store of much-needed weapons, ammunition, and horses. After the destruction of so many homes in Williamsburg, the victory at Black Mingo provided an important boost ~ practical and psychological ~ to the Patriot cause in eastern South Carolina.

Erected: 2012 by Francis Marion Trail Commission of Francis Marion University.

Date visited: _____

Comments: _____

_____

_____

Pee Dee
Region 3 Site 38

Occupation of Georgetown*

33.36715°N 79.28276°W

July 1, 1780–January 24, 1781

Georgetown County

Result: Patriot victory

Combatants	
Loyalist militia	Patriot militia
Commanders and Leaders	
Lt. Col. George Campbell	Brig. Gen. Francis Marion
	Lt. Col. Henry "Light Horse Harry" Lee
Strength	
200–300	Approx 350
Casualties and Losses	
1 killed	1 killed
3 captured	2 wounded

American Capts. Patrick Carnes and Michael Rudolph of Lee's Legion moved down the Pee Dee River on the tide on boats and concealed their men until nightfall. They landed at Mitchell Point and easily penetrated into British held Georgetown under cover of darkness. The Americans rushed into the British Headquarters to capture Lt. Col. George Campbell without firing a shot. Lt. Col. Campbell was staying at the extant house at 222 Broad Street. Patriot Lt. James Cryer and his men surrounded a tavern that contained Maj. Matthew Irvine and Adjutant John Crookshank, believed to be the extant house at 719 Prince Street. Irvine rushed out of the tavern and was killed by Lt. Cryer with his bayonet since Irvine had him given 500 lashes. Lt. Cryer then turned to bayonet Crookshank, but the tavern keeper's daughter begged for his life so Maj. Crookshank was taken prisoner. When South Carolina Patriot militia Brig. Gen. Francis Marion arrived by land as the second prong of the attack, not a British soldier could be found in Georgetown as they had all retreated to the brick jail and redoubt that Marion determined was too strong to take without artillery.

*Marker

ATTACKS UPON GEORGETOWN

On January 24, 1781 Capts. Carnes and Rudulph, by orders from Gen. Marion and Col. Lee, surprised the British garrison at Georgetown and captured Col. Campbell. Upon Gen. Marion's second approach, June 6, 1781, the British evacuated the town. Gen. Marion seized the stores, demolished the works, and retired.

Date visited: _____

Comments: _____

_____

_____

Pee Dee
Region 3 Site 39

Battle of Kingstree*

September 6, 1780

33.40359°N 79.50406°W

Williamsburg County

Result: Patriot victory

Combatants	
Loyalist militia	Patriot militia
Commanders and Leaders	
Maj. James Wemyss	Maj. John James
Strength	
unknown	unknown
Casualties and Losses	
30 killed or captured	5 killed
	15 wounded
	10 captured

British Maj. James Wemyss was sent to Williamsburg Township (Kingstree) by Lord Cornwallis to organize a Loyalist militia and put down the Patriots in the area. He was ordered to seize arms and ammunition and punish those hiding them. South Carolina Patriot militia Col. Francis Marion sent Maj. John James with a small force to determine the strength of the British and Loyalist militia. James counted the crown force as they marched by. As the rear guard started to pass, James attacked, killing or capturing 30 British troops. James quickly fled the scene, but lost 5 killed, 15 wounded and 10 captured.

Note: The historical marker has the wrong date. Wemyss passed through Kingstree about September 6, 1780. This date is based on Marion's letters giving the dates for Blue Savannah and other actions.

*Marker

BATTLE OF KINGSTREE

Somewhere northwest of Kingstree on the night of Aug. 27, 1780, while scouting for Gen. Marion. A South Carolina militia company led by Maj. John James attacked a British force sent to ravage Williamsburg District, capturing prisoners and gaining information that decided Gen. Marion not to risk a general engagement.

Erected: 1958 by Margaret Gregg Gordon Chapter, D.A.R., Williamsburg County.

Date visited: _____

Comments: _____

_____

_____

Lowcountry Region

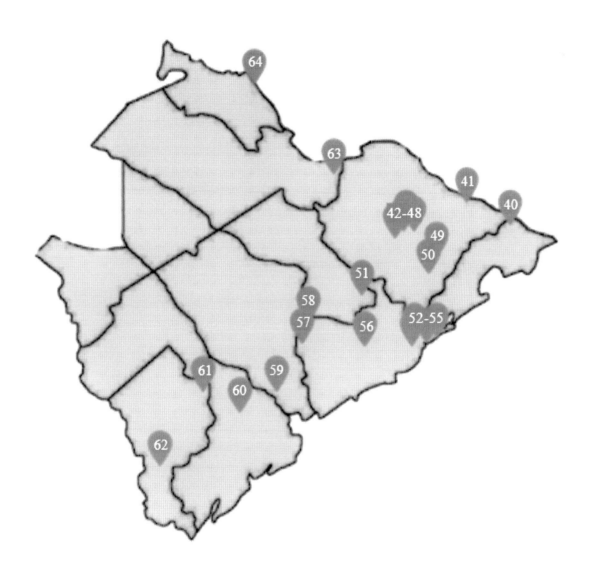

Lowcountry
Region IV

Site #	Location	County	Date
40.	Battle of Wambaw Bridge	Charleston/Berkeley	February 24, 1782
41.	Battle of Lenud's Ferry*	Berkeley	May 6, 1780
42.	Battle of Biggin Bridge	Berkeley	April 14, 1780
			July 16, 1781
43.	Ruins of Biggin Church*	Berkeley	April 14, 1780
44.	Battle of Moncks Corner*	Berkeley	April 14, 1780
45.	Fairlawn Barony/		
	Colleton Mansion*	Berkeley	April 14, 1780–
			November 17, 1781
46.	Battle of Wadboo Bridge	Berkeley	January 31, 1781
47.	Fort Fairlawn*	Berkeley	November 17, 1781
48.	Avenue of Cedars	Berkeley	August 29, 1782
49.	Battle of Quinby Bridge*	Berkeley	July 17, 1781
50.	Battle of Videau's Bridge	Berkeley	January 3, 1782
51.	Battle of Fort Dorchester*	Dorchester	July 14, 1781
			December 1, 1781
52.	Breach Inlet Action*/		
	Battle of Fort Sullivan		
	(Fort Moultrie)	Charleston	June 18–June 28, 1776
			June 28, 1776
53.	Siege of Charleston*		
	Fall of Charleston	Charleston	March 29–
			May 12, 1780
54.	Site of Hanging Isaac Hayne*		
	(Isaac Hayne's Gravesite)	Charleston	August 4, 1781
55.	Battle of James Island		
	(Dill's Bluff)	Charleston	November 14, 1782
56.	Battle of Stono Ferry	Charleston	June 20, 1779
57.	Jacksonborough—*		
	Provisional Capital of SC	Colleton	January–
			February, 1782

58.	Battle of Parker's Ferry*	Colleton	August 30, 1781
59.	Battle of Tar Bluff (Combahee Ferry)	Colleton	August 27, 1782
60.	Battle of Port Royal Island*	Beaufort	February 2–3, 1779
61.	Battle of Coosawhatchie Bridge*	Jasper	May 3, 1779
62.	Site of Purrysburg	Jasper	April 29, 1779
63.	Battle of Eutaw Springs*	Orangeburg	September 8, 1781
64.	Siege of Fort Motte	Calhoun	May 8–12, 1781

Lowcountry
Region 4 Site 40

Battle of Wambaw Bridge

33.20742°N 79.46878°W

February 24, 1782

Charleston/ Berkeley County

Result: British victory

Combatants	
Great Britain	United States
Commanders and Leaders	
Lt. Col. Benjamin Thompson	Lt. Col. Archibald McDonald
Strength	
700	500
Casualties and Losses	
40 killed	10 killed
4 captured	8 wounded

Patriot Col. Peter Horry was put in charge of Brig. Gen. Marion's brigade while Brig. Gen. Marion was in the General Assembly meeting in Jacksonboro. Col. Horry followed Gen. Marion's advice and moved the brigade to Wambaw Creek near the Santee River where forage was available and the brigade would be more secure from harassment by the British. British Lt. Col. Benjamin Thompson set out from Daniel Island with a British expedition consisting of the cavalry and mounted militia to engage Marion's brigade. He was detected early on, but Col. Horry was absent dining across the river at this plantation; however, he had given command to Col. Archibald McDonald. The officers who were warned of the enemy approach did not believe the reports, so the Patriots were taken by surprise when the attack commenced late in the afternoon. The Americans broke and fled as the Loyalist militia charged. The action started at the bridge and finished about 100 yards beyond the bridge in Berkeley County.

Date visited: _____

Comments: _____

_____

_____

Lowcountry
Region 4 Site 41

Battle of Lenud's Ferry*

33.29441°N 79.68673°W

May 6, 1780

Berkeley County

Result: British victory

Combatants	
Great Britain Loyalist militia	United States
Commanders and Leaders	
Lt. Col. Banastre Tarleton	Col. Anthony Walton White Lt. Col. William Washington
Strength	
150	350
Casualties and Losses	
2 killed 4 horses killed	45 killed and wounded

After their rout at Biggin Church, the remnants of the American cavalry assembled on the north side of the Santee River under Col. Anthony Walton White. After a successful harassment of a foraging party on the south side of the river, White's men were delayed in crossing the river back to the north side waiting for the Virginia Continentals on the opposite bank to assist them. Lt. Col. Banastre Tarleton learned of their location from a Loyalist informer, made a rapid pursuit, and took White's forces by surprise at the ferry. The loss of men and horses demoralized the Patriots and severely curtailed their operations for some months.

*Marker
Battle of Lenud's Ferry

Here, on May 6, 1780, Col. A.M. White was routed by Tarleton with the loss of two officers and thirty-six men killed and wounded and seven officers and sixty dragoons taken; Tarleton

lost 2 men. Two boys, Francis Deliesseline and Samuel Dupre, recaptured fourteen of White's horses and delivered them to Maj. Jamison, Georgetown, refusing reward.

Erected: by Berkeley County Historical Society.

Date visited: _____

Comments: _____

_____

_____

**Lowcountry
Region 4 Site 42**

Battle of Biggin Bridge

33.21171°N   79.97880°W

April 14, 1780

Berkeley County

Result: British victory

Combatants	
Great Britain	United States
Commanders and Leaders	
Lt. Col. Banastre Tarleton	Gen. Isaac Huger
Maj. Patrick Ferguson	Lt. Col. William Washington
Strength	
1,400	500
Casualties and Losses	
3 wounded	15 killed
	18 wounded
	63 missing or captured

The American militia cavalry, commanded by Gen. Isaac Huger and Lt. Col. William Washngton, were posted at Monck's Corner to guard the Biggin Bridge. In the early morning hours of April 14, British Lt. Col. Banastre Tarleton and Maj. Patrick Ferguson, leading the advance of a British detachment surprised the American cavalry, forced the passage over Biggin Bridge, and routed the militia on the opposite bank. Tarleton not only achieved an important strategic victory, but he also captured four hundred horses badly needed by his cavalry, whose mounts had been lost on the voyage from New York due to a severe storm at sea.

Date visited: _____

Comments: _____

_____

_____

Lowcountry
Region 4 Site 43

Ruins of Biggin Church*

33.21240°N 79.96671°W

April 14, 1780

Berkeley County

Result: British victory

Combatants	
Great Britain	United States
Loyalist militia	
Commanders and Leaders	
Lt. Col. John Coates	Brig. Gen. Thomas Sumter
Strength	
500	Approx. 500
Casualties and Losses	
6 killed	30 killed
38 wounded	30 wounded
100 captured	

South Carolina militia commander Brig. Gen. Thomas Sumter, with Col. Edward Lacey, were directing operations against the fortified British post at Biggin Church. British Lt. Col. James Coates occupied the brick church with his 19th Regiment and mounted infantry of the Loyalist South Carolina Rangers. Patriot Col. Peter Horry and his men camped at Wadboo Bridge all day. About five o'clock in the afternoon, British Maj. Thomas Fraser advanced with the South Carolina Rangers and charged the Patriots in their camp. Horry's men, caught by surprise, rallied, counterattacked with Col. Edward Lacey's mounted riflemen, and drove the British back to their lines. The Americans took several prisoners; one was discovered to have been a Patriot and was executed for his treason. The Rangers' charge was a delaying action for Lt. Col. Coates, as he then put all of his stores into Biggin Church, burned it in the middle of the night and retreated toward Charleston.

*Marker
Biggin Church

Parish Church of St. John's Berkeley, founded by Act of Assembly November 30, 1706. Church erected in 1712. Burned by forest fire in 1775 and restored. Burned by Col. Coates of the British Army in 1781 and again restored. Burned again by forest fire about 1886. Gen. William Moultrie and Henry Laurens were among the vestrymen of the parish.

Date visited: _____

Comments: _____

_____

_____

Lowcountry
Region 4 Site 44

Battle of Moncks Corner*

33.12187°N 79.59335°W

April 14, 1780

Berkeley County

Result: British victory

Combatants	
Great Britain	United States Patriot militia
Commanders and Leaders	
Lt. Col. Banastre Tarleton	Brig. Gen. Isaac Huger
Strength	
Approx. 1,400	500
Casualties and Losses	
3 wounded	15 killed 18 wounded 63 captured

As part of his preparations for the Siege of Charlestown, on April 12, 1780, General Sir Henry Clinton ordered Lt. Col. Banastre Tarleton into the countryside to cut off the city's lines of communication. On the night of April 13, he approached Moncks Corner by night march. In the early morning hours of April 14th, Lt. Col. Tarleton caught the Patriot forces there completely by surprise and quickly routed them.

From ten o'clock on the night of April 13, 1780, a swift, silent march was undertaken along the road to Moncks Corner by Lt. Col. Banastre Tarleton and his men. They encountered no American scouts or patrols. When they reached Moncks Corner, they caught the Patriots completely by surprise. Not only had there been no patrols, but Brigadier General Isaac Huger had placed his cavalry in front of his infantry.

Lt. Col. Tarleton led a charge right at the Patriots since swamps on either side precluded a flank attack. The British easily dispersed the militia defending Biggin Bridge. Many of the Patriots were able to escape, including Brigadier General Isaac Huger and Lt. Col. William Washington, who had suffered yet another defeat by Lt. Col. Banastre Tarleton. Lt. Col. Tarleton was also able to capture wagons of supplies and a great many excellent cavalry horses.

The Continental defeat at Moncks Corner left Major General Benjamin Lincoln without any lines of communication from Charlestown. The Patriots also lost many of their decent horses for cavalry use, setting them back considerably. This defeat only hastened the surrender of Charlestown.

*Marker
First Site of Moncks Corner

First site of Monck's Corner, where the road to the Congarees branched off from this road. Founded by Thomas Monck in 1735. Relocated on the railroad about 1856.

Here about 3:30 A.M. April 13, 1780, Col. Wm. Washington's Light Dragoons were surprised by a superior force of the British under Lt. Cols. Webster and Tarleton and Maj. Ferguson. Maj. Vernier, of Pulaski's Legion, and 25 men were killed and the Americans routed. The British fortified the place, but in July 1781, abandoned the redoubt here and fell back to the parish church which had been fortified.

Date visited: _____

Comments: _____

_____

_____

Lowcountry
Region 4 Site 45

Fairlawn Barony*
(Colleton Mansion)
November 17, 1781

33.18762 °N 79.99239 °W

Berkeley County

Result: Patriot victory

Combatants	
Great Britain	United States
Commanders and Leaders	
Capt. Murdock MacLaine	Lt. Col. Hezekiah Maham
	Col. Isaac Shelby
Strength	
50	200
Casualties and Losses	
150 sick and wounded captured	unknown

South Carolina Patriot Brig. Gen. Francis Marion dispatched about 200 troops under Lt. Col. Hezekiah Maham and Col. Isaac Shelby with his "over-the-mountain" men to get behind the main British army and strike at the Fair Lawn Barony's "Colleton Mansion," since the enemy force there had been reduced. The "Colleton Mansion" was being used as a hospital for British troops and an earthen redoubt about half a mile from the house guarded the nearby Cooper River landing. This redoubt was garrisoned by 50 troops of the British 84th Regiment under Capt. Murdock MacLaine. On approach to Fair Lawn, some of Lt. Col. Maham's riflemen were ordered to dismount and move as infantry. The occupants of the house were given the choice of either surrendering or having their works stormed by Shelby's tomahawk-wielding mountaineers. No resistance was made and surrender took place. In the house was found 300 stands of srms, many stores of value, some sick and 80 wounded convalescents carried off on horseback as prisoners. The house with its remaining contents was burned.

Note: There is debate as to whether the Americans or British set fire to the "Colleton Mansion." It was burned, but the British claim it was burned by the Americans, and the Americans claim the British burned it. The issue of who actually burned the house has never been resolved.

*Marker
Fort Fairlawn

In April 1780, after their victory at Moncks Corner, British and Loyalist troops occupied Fairlawn and built an earthwork fort 1/2 mi. E. On November 17, 1781, Patriot militia under Cols. Hezekiah Maham and Isaac Shelby, on orders from Gen. Francis Marion, attacked the outpost commanded by Capt. Neil McLean. They took about 150 prisoners. The house, used as a hospital and storehouse, was burned. Contemporary accounts, however, disagree on which force burned it.

Erected: 2011 by Berkeley County Historical Society and the General Marion's Brigade Chapter, Daughters of the American Revolution.

Date visited: _____

Comments: _____

_____

_____

Lowcountry
Region 4 Site 46

Battle of Wadboo Bridge

33.19577°N 79.95348°W

#1 January 31, 1781
#2 July 16, 1781

Berkeley County

Result: Patriot victory

Combatants	
Great Britain	Patriot militia
Commanders and Leaders	
unknown	Capt. John Postelle
Strength	
unknown	Approx. 150
Casualties and Losses	
unknown	unknown

Battle of Wadboo Bridge 1: January 31, 1781: South Carolina Patriot militia Capt. John Postelle was ordered by Gen. Francis Marion to "burn all British stores of every kind" at Wadboo. Capt. Postelle carried out his orders and destroyed the supplies at Wadboo before moving on to Keithfield [Kitfield] Plantation at Moncks Corner.

Result: Patriot victory

Combatants	
Great Britain	Patriot militia
Commanders and Leaders	
unknown	Col. Hezekiah Maham
Strength	
600	Approx. 60–100
Casualties and Losses	
unknown	unknown

Battle of Wadboo Bridge 2: July 16, 1781: South Carolina Patriot militia Col. Hezekiah Maham was ordered by Gen. Sumter to burn the bridge to hinder British Lt. Col. Coates's movement to Charleston, after the battle of Biggin Church, and to prevent supplies reaching him from Charleston. Col. Maham burned the bridge and also burned two British supply vessels in Wadboo Creek.

Date visited: _____

Comments: _____

_____

_____

Lowcountry
Region 4 Site 47

Fort Fairlawn*

April 14, 1780–November 17, 1781

33.18639°N 79.97734°W

Berkeley County

Fort Fairlawn was built on the edge of the plantation's property. Its key location, at the head of the Cooper River and along both a coastal and inward road, rendered its defense strategically important. This square fort had two-meter-tall walls complete with a moat and a water cistern for soldier's use and easy river access. Portions of the wall and moat can still be seen today.

*Marker

Fairlawn Plantation

Fairlawn Barony, sometimes called "Fair-Lawn," was granted to Peter Colleton, whose father John had been one of the original Lords Proprietors of the Carolina colony. John's grandson John (1679–1754), known as "The Honorable," was a planter and member of the Grand Council and the first Colleton to live in S.C. He built a large brick house here, later described by his granddaughter as "of course very magnificent."

Date visited: _____

Comments: _____

_____

_____

Lowcountry
Region 4 Site 48

Avenue of Cedars

August 29, 1782

33.19714°N 79.94195°W

Berkeley County

Result: Patriot victory

Combatants	
Great Britain	Patriot militia
Commanders and Leaders	
Maj. Thomas Fraser	Gen. Francis Marion
Strength	
100 dragoons	Approx. 50
Casualties and Losses	
4 men and 5 horses killed 6 men wounded 1 man and 3 horses captured	0

British Maj. Thomas Fraser and his cavalry arrived in the vicinity of Moncks Corner and discovered that Francis Marion was encamped only a few miles away, at Wadboo Barony. He decided that the best way to protect his foragers was to take the offensive. Fraser led a force of 100 dragoons to attack the Patriots in their camp. The American cavalry happened to be out on patrol, Gen. Marion, a veteran commander, knew not to fight the British horse in the open, so he deployed his men along a line of huge old cedars that lined the avenue to the castle in Colleton's Wadboo Barony. The British attempted a charge, but Marion's devastating fire from the plantation outbuildings on Marion's left repelled them with the loss of four men and five horses killed, six men wounded, one man, and three horses captured. Among the British dead was Capt. Robert Gillis, and Capt. George Dawkins of the South Carolina Royalists was wounded. The only loss suffered by Marion was his ammunition wagon, which fell into enemy hands as the driver attempted to flee the battlefield. Among the Patriot soldiers who rendered distinguished service on this occasion were Capt. Gavin Witherspoon and the former Loyalist Micajah Ganey, who was now serving under Marion with 40 of his followers after years of fighting Gen. Marion.

On December 15, 1782 Gen. Francis Marion came to the Avenue of Cedars again to say goodbye to his militiamen, instead of attending the British evacuation ceremony in Charlestown. Gen Marion left his troops after these heartfelt words, "In his favourite encampment at Wadboo, and on the sides of the cedar trees, he thanked his officers and men for their many and useful services and bid them a friendly and affectionate farewell. He wishes them a long Continuance of happiness and the Blessing of Peace."

Date visited: ————————————————

Comments: ——————————————————————————————

——————————————————————————————————————

——————————————————————————————————————

Lowcountry
Region 4 Site 49

Battle of Quinby Bridge*

33.5671°N 79.48435°W

July 17, 1781

Berkeley County

Result: British victory

Combatants	
Great Britain	United States
Commanders and Leaders	
Lt. Col. John Coates	Brig. Gen. Thomas Sumter
Strength	
600	555
Casualties and Losses	
6 killed	30 killed
38 wounded	30 wounded
100 captured	

When Brig. Gen. Thomas Sumter's Patriots learned that British Lt. Col. James Coates and his 19th Regiment of Foot (the "Green Howards") had escaped to the south after burning Biggin Church, Lt. Col. Henry Lee and Lt. Col. Henry Hampton led the chase, crossing over Wadboo Bridge which was not fully destroyed (or had been repaired in the night by Coates). After an 18-mile chase, Capt. James Armstrong of Col. Henry Lee's Legion cavalry, with his small troop, charged over the Quinby Creek Bridge, whose planks had been loosened by the British. Coates formed his men just to the west of Quinby Creek. The charge was so furious, it knocked off some of the loosened planks as they crossed, and Coates's men scattered. Now Armstrong and his men were isolated on the west side of the bridge, since the bridge was missing many planks dislodged by his charge. Help came as Capt. James McCauley and some of Marion's infantry were able to make it over the bridge with assistance of Armstrong's dragoons, who ran the artillerymen from the British' "Royal" howitzer aimed at the bridge, and scattered Lt. Col. Coates's rear guard. Lt. Col. Coates's regiment withdrew into the houses of nearby Shubrick's Plantation.

*Marker
Quinby Bridge & Shubrick's Plantation: The Disastrous "Raid of the Dog Days"

In the summer of 1781, with the British hold on the interior of South Carolina significantly weakened, Continental commander Maj. Gen. Nathaniel Greene sent Brig. Gen. Thomas Sumter, with Brig. Gen. Francis Marion and Lt. Col. Henry "Light Horse Harry" Lee, to force the British to abandon the area around Charleston and retreat into the city. As Sumter led a force of nearly a thousand men from Orangeburg, British Col. James Coates evacuated the post at Monck's Corner and began moving his troops toward the safety of Charleston.

On July 17, 1781 near Quinby Bridge, Lee's cavalry captured Coates's rear guard and baggage caravan. A portion of Lee's riders crossed the bridge and clashed with the British infantry ~ loosening so many planks in the process that the rest of Lee's and Marion's forces had to march upstream and cross Quinby Creek at a ford. By that time, the British had taken up a strong position in the main house, outbuildings and slave quarters of Shubrick's Plantation. Against the advice of Marion and Lee, Sumter ordered an assault that quickly turned into a costly stalemate. Marion's Brigade alone reported eight or nine killed and eighteen wounded.

Accustomed to conservative tactics that did not unnecessarily risk their lives, many of Marion's men deserted after the battle, and Marion himself resolved never again to fight under Sumter.

Erected: 2012 by Francis Marion Trail Commission of Francis Marion University.

"The Dog Days of Summer" refers to the time period during the first of June and the middle of August, and references the star Sirius, also known as the "Dog Star."

Date visited: _____

Comments: _____

_____

_____

Lowcountry
Region 4 Site 50

Battle at Videau's Bridge

33.02833°N 79.85416°W

January 3, 1782

Berkeley County

Result: British victory

Combatants	
Great Britain	United States
Commanders and Leaders	
Maj. William Bereton	Col. Richard Richardson
Strength	
360	400
Casualties and Losses	
4 killed	22 killed
14 wounded	
1 captured	

British Maj. William Brereton, with the SC royalists, NY volunteers, and Black Dragoons, was ordered to invade St. Thomas Parish and forage for supplies. After landing on Daniel's Island from a ship in the Wando River, the British crossed the island and Beresford Creek, then moved fourteen miles up the Clements Ferry (AKA Cainhoy) Road and halted at Brabant's plantation about noon. At the same time, Gen. Francis Marion ordered his men to block the British advance. SC Patriot militia Col. Richard Richardson, Jr. led his men north from Cainhoy, reinforced by Capt. John Carraway Smith's cavalry. Richardson's troops engaged the British cavalry led by Capt. Archibald Campbell just north of Videau's Bridge. Smith charged and routed the enemy, but disregarded Marion's orders by continuing to advance until he encountered the large force of British infantry at the bridge. Loyalist Maj. John Coffin attacked the Patriots with a fresh troop of cavalry, and Richardson's forces were thrown into retreat on the long, narrow causeway. During the subsequent six-mile pursuit by the British, several of Gen. Marion's soldiers distinguished themselves by heroic actions. However, the Americans were defeated.

Date visited: _____

Comments: _____

_____

_____

Lowcountry
Region 4 Site 51

Battle of Fort Dorchester*

#1 July 14, 1781

#2 December 1, 1781

32.94833°N 80.16979°W

Berkeley County

Result: Patriot victory

Combatants	
Great Britain	United States Patriot militia
Commanders and Leaders	
Lt. David Waugh	Lt. Col. Wade Hampton
Strength	
unknown	Approx. 1,200
Casualties and Losses	
unknown	unknown

Battle of Fort Dorchester #1: July 14, 1781: American Lt. Col. Henry "Light Horse Harry" Lee was assigned to take Dorchester and then press on to "thunder" at the gates of Charlestown. Contrary to expectations, Lee met no resistance at Fort Dorchester. The garrison had been greatly reduced by the draft made on it by Lt. Col. Alexander Stewart and by a mutiny, during which it was said that many were killed and wounded. The sudden appearance of Lt. Col. Wade Hampton at Goose Creek Bridge alarmed the garrison at Fort Dorchester, and in their demoralized condition, they abandoned the fort. However, Col. Lee arrived in time to seize as many as 200 horses, four wagons, three of which were empty, but the fourth wagon contained a much-needed supply of powder and shot.

Result: Patriot victory

Combatants	
Great Britain	United States
Commanders and Leaders	
Lt. Maj. John Doyle	Maj. Gen. Nathanael Greene
Strength	
850	400
Casualties and Losses	
10 killed	0 killed
20 wounded	unknown wounded

Battle of Fort Dorchester #2: December 1, 1781: Pennsylvania Continental reinforcements, after the fall of Yorktown, Virginia, enabled American Gen. Nathanael Greene to move his headquarters into the lower part of the state and drive the British into Charleston. On November 18, 1781, he broke camp at the High Hills of Santee and began his march southward. From Fort Motte on November 30, Gen. Greene led his mounted troops ahead of the main army, intending to strike the British Fort at Dorchester. However, Loyalist sympathizers informed the British and so eliminated the element of surprise. On December 1, 1781, the British sent out a reconnoitering party on the west side of the Ashley River, which encountered the American vanguard under Lt. Col. Wade Hampton. The British were driven back across Dorchester Creek Bridge with the loss of 8 or 10 killed and 15 or 20 wounded. The British took cover at Fort Dorchester, but the cavalry sallied out of the fort and Hampton's troops quickly chased them back into the fort. The British garrison made its escape under the cover of darkness, burning all military stores and throwing the cannons into the Ashley River. The British retreated to the Quarter House, about 5 miles from Charlestown, where they rendezvoused with the main British army.

*Marker
Fort Dorchester

A brick powder magazine enclosed by a tabby wall eight feet high was built here in 1757. During the Revolution, Dorchester was a strategic point. In 1775 the magazine was fortified and the garrison commanded by Capt. Francis Marion. British troops occupied the town in

April 1780. They were driven out by cavalry and infantry under Col. Wade Hampton and Gen. Nathanael Greene on December 1, 1781.

Erected: 1963 by S.C. State Commission of Forestry, Division of State Parks.

Date visited: _____

Comments: _____

_____

_____

Lowcountry
Region 4 Site 52

Breach Inlet Action*

June 18–28, 1776

32.77490°N   79.81440°W

Charleston County

Result: Patriot victory

Combatants	
Great Britain	United States
Commanders and Leaders	
Maj. Gen. Sir Henry Clinton	Col. William Thomson
Strength	
3,000	780
Casualties and Losses	
100 killed	1 killed
51 wounded	4 wounded

The British Army landed unopposed on the north end of Long Island (now Isle of Palms) in early June 1776. On June 21st, the Americans fired several cannon shots at the armed schooner, *Lady William*, and a sloop. Several rounds hulled them. When the royal Navy began its bombardment of Sullivan's Fort (Fort Moultrie), Maj. Gen. Sir Henry Clinton, on the Isle of Palms, made ready for crossing Breach Inlet with 3,000 redcoats to attack the 780 Americans commanded by American Col. William "Old Danger" Thomson defending the northern end of Sullivan's Island. Clinton's troops marched to the inlet and boarded their flat boats and small craft. On Clinton's right flank were a sloop and the armed schooner, *Lady William,* to support their crossing. On Clinton's left flank was the sloop, *Ranger*. The British boats did get close enough to have their decks cleared by grapeshot, after which they dispersed. By this time the tide had come in and the Inlet could not be forded. The British Army retired and left the battle to the Royal Navy, which could not dislodge the Americans. This action is often overlooked, but was a major factor in defeating the British plan to capture Charleston in 1776.

*Marker
Ten days of skirmishing on beaches, creeks, and marshes climaxed on June 28, 1776 with the British attempt to cross Breach Inlet during the bombardment of Fort Sullivan. Colonel

William "Danger" Thompson and 780 American Patriots had dug trenches and erected two fortifications of palmetto logs to protect this end of Sullivan's Island.

After extensive scouting, maneuvering, and fighting, the British generals realized that crossing the treacherous and well-defended inlet would be dangerous. Nonetheless, they sent hundreds of men in 15 armed flatboats across the inlet supported by warships, artillery, and infantry. The Americans repelled the attack and defeated the British army of 3,000.

Meanwhile, 435 American soldiers under the command of Colonel William Moultrie held Fort Sullivan in a dramatic, day-long battle against the British navy. The story of their heroic defense is told at Fort Moultrie.

Battle of Fort Sullivan
1. Battle of Fort Sullivan Marker—Side A
Inscription. Click to hear the inscription.
[Side A]
On June 28, 1776, a British and Loyalist force seeking to capture Charleston advanced to Sullivan's Island with 9 ships and 2,500–3,000 infantry. The American defenders, 435 men under Col. William Moultrie of the 2nd S.C. Regiment, occupied a fort nearby, built from plametto logs. Still unfinished when the fighting began, it is sometimes referred to as "Fort Sullivan" in contemporary accounts.

[Side B]
As Adm. Peter Parker's ships shelled the fort its log walls absorbed or deflected the British shells and the Americans lost only 37 men killed or wounded. Moultrie's shells damaged every ship, inflicted 219 losses, and forced Parker's withdrawal. A British land attack at Breach Inlet also failed. The first major Patriot victory of the war also gave S.C. its nickname, "The Palmetto State."

Erected: 2005 by Fort Sullivan Chapter, National Society of the Daughters of the American Revolution.

Date visited: _____

Comments: _____

_____

_____

Lowcountry
Region 4 Site 53

Battle at Fort Moultrie

June 28, 1776

32.75911°N 79.85810°W

Charleston County

Result: Patriot victory

Combatants	
Great Britain Loyalist militia	United States
Commanders and Leaders	
Adm. Peter Parker	Col. William Moultrie
Strength	
3,000	435
Casualties and Losses	
91 killed	12 killed
170 wounded	24 wounded

A British and Loyalist force seeking to capture Charleston advanced to Sullivan's Island with 9 ships and 2,500–3,000 infantry. The American defenders, 435 men under Col. William Moultrie of the 2nd SC Regiment, occupied a fort nearby, built from palmetto logs. Still unfinished when the fighting began, it is sometimes referred to as "Fort Sullivan" in contemporary accounts. During the British bombardment, the flagstaff at the fort was shot down and a young officer by the name of Sgt. William Jasper risked his life to hold the flagstaff aloft until a new one could be installed while the British continued to fire on the fort.

As Adm. Peter Parker's ships shelled the fort, its log walls absorbed or deflected the British shells and the Americans lost only 37 men, killed or wounded. Moultrie's shells damaged every ship, inflicted 219 losses, and forced Parker's withdrawal. A British land attack at Breach Inlet also failed. Had the British been able to ford to the other side and land, the outcome of the battle may have been different. The back of Fort Sullivan was not completed and if the British could have crossed they could have taken Fort Sullivan/Fort Moultrie. The first major Patriot victory of the war also gave SC its nickname "The Palmetto State."

Date visited: _____

Comments: _____

_____

_____

Lowcountry
Region 4 Site 53

Siege of Charleston/*
Fall of Charleston

March 29–May 12, 1780

32.78673°N 79.93633°W

Charleston County

Result: British victory

Combatants		
	Great Britain	United States
	Loyalist militia	Patriot militia
Commanders and Leaders		
	Gen. Sir Henry Clinton	Maj. Gen. Benjamin Lincoln
Strength		
	12,847	6,577
Casualties and Losses		
	99 killed	89 killed
	217 wounded	138 wounded
	Approx. 7 captured	3,371 captured

On March 20, 1780, the British Admiral Marriott Arbuthnot crossed the Charleston Bar unopposed after many days of being at the mercy of the wind. By March 27, Maj. Gen. Benjamin Lincoln, commander of the American forces, realized that his navy would not fight. On March 29, under the cover of fog, the first of the British crossed the Ashley River at Benjamin Fuller's plantation and proceeded toward Charleston. The British dug trenches north of the American defensive wall and the Hornwork, which was a fortification inside the wall. The trenches, or parallels, were moved closer and closer to the American lines by digging perpendicular trenches, until Maj. Gen. Lincoln realized that continuing the fight would only result in more loss of life both in the city, which was under cannon fire, and of his troops. After days of cannon bombardment and skirmishing Lincoln surrendered the Southern Patriot Army and the City of Charleston to the British on May 12, 1780.

*Marker
The Siege of Charleston, 1780

The British capture of Charleston in May 1780 was one of the worst American defeats of the Revolution. On March 30–31 Gen. Henry Clinton's British, Hessian, and Loyalist force crossed the Ashley River north of Charleston. On April 1 Clinton advanced against the American lines near this site, held by Gen. Benjamin Lincoln's Continentals and militia. The 42-day siege would be the longest of the war.

As Gen. Charles Cornwallis closed off Lincoln's escape routes on the Cooper River, Clinton advanced his siege lines and bombarded Charleston. On May 12, 1780, in front of the American works near this spot, Lincoln surrendered the city and his force of 6,000 men, after what one British officer called "a gallant defense." The British occupied Charleston for more than 2 1/2 years, evacuating Dec. 14, 1782.

Erected: 2010 by The South Carolina Societies of the Daughters of the American Revolution and Sons of the American Revolution, and the Maj. Gen. William Moultrie Chapter, Sons of the American Revolution.

Date visited: _____

Comments: _____

_____

_____

Lowcountry
Region 4 Site 54

Hanging Isaac Hayne*
(Isaac Hayne's Gravesite)
August 4, 1781

32.80691°N 80.47918°W

Charleston County

South Carolina Patriot militia Col. Hayne had captured Gen. Andrew Williamson on July 15, 1781, after taking parole and protection from the British. This act made him a marked man by the British, who immediately began to hunt him down. He was captured later in July and taken to Charleston for trial. The trial was swift and he was found guilty of violating his parole. His hanging spawned several retaliation raids by the Americans.

*Marker
ISAAC HAYNE THE MARTYR
Captured near here by the British in July 1781, while commanding a party of militia. Col. Hayne was taken to Charleston. Imprisoned in the Exchange Building, and hanged by his conquerors as a traitor on August 4, 1781, having previously laid down his arms to be with his family who were ill with smallpox. By his death he became a martyr for liberty.
Martyr Of The Revolution / Hayne Hall

Martyr Of The Revolution
When Loyalists soldiers attacked the camp of Col. Isaac Hayne's S.C. militia about 5 mi. W on July 7, 1781, they captured Hayne. He was soon condemned as a traitor because he had previously declared allegiance to Great Britain after the fall of Charleston. Hayne, hanged in Charleston on August 4, 1781, became a martyr to those fighting for America's independence.

Hayne Hall
The surrounding land was part of Hayne Hall plantation, home of the Hayne Family in South Carolina and Colonel Isaac Hayne
(Sept. 23, 1745 ~ Aug. 4, 1781).

Rice planter, iron manufacturer, church leader and Patriot soldier, Colonel Hayne was executed by the British during the Revolution and buried here in the family cemetery.

Erected: 2007 by the South Carolina Department of Parks, Recreation and Tourism, State Park Service, replacing a marker erected in 1964.

Fateful Choices—The Hanging Of Isaac Hayne
Isaac Hayne tried to spend the rest of the Revolutionary War in peace after the British captured Charleston in 1780. Although he had supported independence, Hayne accepted a parole—a promise to remain neutral—in exchange for his freedom. But the British soon forced him to choose sides and declare his alleigiance to them.

In 1781, with the British losing the war, Hayne returned to the fight for independence, only to be captured after leading a raid. Desparate to keep other paroled Patriots from taking up arms again, the British executed Hayne after a trial by military tribunal.

Erected: by South Carolina State Park Service.

Date visited: _____

Comments: _____

_____

_____

Lowcountry
Region 4 Site 55

Battle at James Island
(Dill's Bluff)
November 14, 1782

32.74712°N 79.944731°W

Berkeley County

Result: British victory

Combatants	
Great Britain	United States
Commanders and Leaders	
Maj. William Dansey	Col. Thaddeus Kosciusko
Strength	
300	70
Casualties and Losses	
2 killed	5 killed
3 wounded	5 wounded

South Carolina Patriot militia Capt. William Wlimot discovered that a party of 50 to 100 British sailors were landing at Dill's Bluff every morning about sunrise for the purpose of cutting wood. Continental Col. Thaddeus Kosciusko and Wilmot crossed to the island that night and lay in ambush for the enemy the following morning. However, the woodcutters failed to appear. The British had learned of the ambush and the military escort for the woodcutters was increased from 20 men to a substantial force of infantry and cavalry. This guard force was based at Fort Johnson under the command of British Maj. William Dansey of the 33rd Regiment. The Americans were persuaded to make a second attempt on the British woodcutters about three weeks later. Relying on a false intelligence report, Kosciusko, Wilmot, and Lt. John Markland crossed to the island with a force of 50 or 60 soldiers of Maryland and Pennsylvania Continentals. They engaged the covering force upon its arrival, but discovered that the British were ready for them. British reinforcements were rapidly advanced to the scene until at least 300 men and one field piece confronted the Patriots. Kosciusko withdrew after a hard-fought action, leaving a number of casualties on the field. Wilmot was killed and Lt. Moore of the Maryland line was mortally wounded. Another American casualty was a slave named William Smith, who was wounded and taken prisoner by the British. Kosciusko was unharmed, although four musket balls pierced his coat and a short lance was shattered in his hand. He narrowly escaped being cut down by a British dragoon, but was saved by a young volunteer named William Fuller. This is said to be the last land battle of the Revolution in South Carolina.

Date visited: _____

Comments: _____

_____

_____

Lowcountry
Region 4 Site 56

Battle at Stono Ferry

June 20, 1779

32.74990°N 80.16245°W

Charleston County

Result: British victory

Combatants	
Great Britain	United States
Commanders and Leaders	
Lt. Col. John Maitland	Maj. Gen. Benjamin Lincoln
Strength	
800	1,200
Casualties and Losses	
26 killed	34 killed
93 wounded	115 wounded
	155 missing

Shortly after midnight on June 20, 1779, Patriot Maj. Gen. Benjamin Lincoln and most of his troops left camp, dragging several small pieces of field artillery. Lincoln mistakenly formed the lines three-quarters of a mile away from the enemy, due to his poor knowledge of the land between his position and the British. At about seven in the morning the Patriots started advancing, with the North Carolina militia on the right slowed by a pine thicket. After engaging some British Highlander pickets, the battle began on the Patriot right and quickly spread to the left. An unexpected creek and marsh stopped the Patriots advance. At the creek, they were exposed to the fire of the enemy, who were under the cover of their fortifications. The Patriots on the right and left apparently got within 60 yards of the British fortifications. The militia, on the right, almost overran the Hessians, but was driven back by cannon fire from the British galley in the river. The Patriots' small 3-pound cannons proved useless against the redoubts and they could not draw the British into open combat. Lincoln called for a retreat when he saw the causeway to the ferry on Johns Island, which is three fourth of a mile long and twenty-eight feet wide, was completely covered, from the woods down to the river, with British reinforcements. The retreat was orderly, with the casualties being carried off the field. About 115 Patriot soldiers were wounded and 155 were missing. In spite of the defeat, the survivors left the field convinced they would have been victorious had the British come out for open combat. Although the British won, they soon left Stono Ferry to continue their island hopping withdrawal back to Savannah from the Charleston area.

Date visited: _____

Comments: _____

_____

_____

**Lowcountry
Region 4 Site 57**

Jacksonborough—
Provincial Capital of SC*

32.76983°N 80.45350°W

January–February, 1782

Colleton County

On the eighth of January, 1782, the British were in firm control of Charlestown, which they had captured in May of 1780. That same day, a mere thirty miles westward, the General Assembly of South Carolina's Revolutionary government convened in their capitol, Jacksonborough, little more than a settlement on the Edisto River. By February 26th, they had formulated and passed several Confiscation Acts. The lists of names—some of them misspelled—accompanying the Acts were printed in the March 20, 1782 issue of Charlestown's Royal Gazette. The list would be revised several times by the war's end.

*Marker
Old Jacksonborough

Founded about 1735 on lands granted John Jackson in 1701; county seat of Colleton District from 1799 to 1822. Provisional capital of state while Charleston was under siege in the closing months of the American Revolution. First South Carolina Legislature met here Jan.–Feb. 1782. Sessions held in Masonic Lodge and Tavern. Passed Confiscation and Amercement Acts.

Erected: 1959 by Colleton County Historical Society.

Date visited: _____

Comments: _____
_____
_____

Lowcountry
Region 4 Site 58

Battle of Parker's Ferry*

August 30, 1781

32.85087°N 80.41628°W

Colleton County

Result: Patriot victory

Combatants	
Great Britain	United States
Commanders and Leaders	
Lt. Col. Ernst Von Borck	Brig. Gen. Francis Marion
Strength	
660	445
Casualties and Losses	
125 killed	1 killed
80 wounded	3 wounded

South Carolina Patriot Brig. Gen. Francis Marion, with about 180 men, made a hard ride of at least 100 miles, crossed Edisto River, and joined South Carolina Patriot militia Col. William Harden at his Round O camp. After receiving reinforcements from the local militia, Marion placed his men in a swamp next to the road about 1 mile from Parker's Ferry. Marion anticipated the British moving northeast from their camp at Col. Isaac Hayne's home, Hayne Hall, after an unsuccessful attempt at the British foraging party at Godfrey's Savannah. About sunset, while the Patriots were waiting in the swamp for the main British force, a small party of Tories crossed the Edisto River at the ferry and in passing, one of them yelled that he saw a white feather and fired his gun. This caused an exchange of a few shots by both sides, and gave up Marion's element of surprise. Marion detached 15 dragoons to chase the Tories back across Edisto River. The British commander, (Hessian) Lt. Col. Ernst L. Von Borck, marching towards Marion's chosen ambush site about one mile away, thinking that only Col. Harden's party was in the swamp, dispatched his cavalry under Maj. Thomas Fraser to the head of his column to route Harden's men. Fraser's South Carolina Provincials arrived in full charge within 40 or 50 yards of, and parallel to, Marion's ambush. The deadly fire from the swamp made Fraser realize that a greater force than Harden's was in the swamp. Fraser could only "run the gauntlet" of Marion's fire, which exposed his men to more fire from Marion; they were slowed by the fallen horses and were wedged on the narrow causeway so closely that every shot had a devastating effect. Fraser was unhorsed and trampled. Lt. Col. Von Borck soon arrived with his infantry and artillery and attacked Marion's men in the swamp. Marion's sharpshooters picked off the British artillerymen who were unable to fire their cannon. After a few minutes, it appeared that Marion's position might be flanked, and with darkness increasing, Marion's men withdrew a few hundred yards. Borck, seeing an opportunity to disengage, withdrew his troops and Marion took the road for three hours. This ambush took place on the long low-lying road to Parker's Ferry. The next morning, finding the Parker's Ferry Road occupied by the British, Marion's men returned to Round O and re-crossed the Edisto River to rejoin Gen. Nathanael Greene prior to the Battle of Eutaw Springs. This action denied British Lt. Col. Alexander Stewart many cavalrymen one week later at his defense of Eutaw Springs.

*Marker
Battle Of Parker's Ferry

Sent to intercept a raid by 540 Hessians, British, and Tories, General Francis Marion with a force of 400 men on August 30, 1781 set up an ambuscade along this road about 1 mile from the ferry. The enemy advancing along the narrow causeway were surprised and suffered heavy losses, forcing them to withdraw to Charles Town.

Erected: 1961 by Colleton County Historical Society.

Date visited: _____

Comments: _____

_____

_____

Lowcountry
Region 4 Site 59

Battle at Tar Bluff
(Combahee Ferry)

August 27, 1782

32.58494°N 80.57792°W

Colleton County

Result: Patriot victory

Combatants	
Great Britain	United States
Loyalist militia	
Commanders and Leaders	
Maj. William Brereton	Brig. Gen. Mordecai Gist
Strength	
500	500
Casualties and Losses	
1 killed	2 killed
7 wounded	19 wounded

British Gen. Alexander Leslie dispatched a foraging expedition south from Charleston, consisting of 300 British regulars, and 200 Loyalists under the command of Maj. William Brereton of the 64th Regiment. This force sailed to the Combahee River in a fleet totaling 18 vessels, consisting of 2 row galleys, the *Balfour* and the *Shark*, some topsail schooners, and various smaller craft. American Maj. Gen. Nathanael Greene ordered Brig. Gen. Mordecai Gist to protect the rice plantations along the Combahee River. Col. John Laurens, although ill with a fever, hurried after Gist and overtook his brigade near Combahee Ferry. On the morning of August 27, Laurens was stationed just south of Tar Bluff (Combahee Bluff) to confront the enemy flotilla on its return trip down the river from Combahee Ferry. The Americans employed their howitzer so effectively that the British found their retreat cut off and were forced to send a party ashore to silence the American battery. Maj. Brereton landed a large force of infantry with elements of the 17th and 64th Regiments and a detachment of provincials, amounting to at least 140 and possibly as many as 300 men. Laurens withdrew to the high ground north of the battery and boldly decided to deploy his troops and engage the British superior numbers instead of waiting for Gist's reinforcements. The results was a disaster for the Americans. Laurens was caught in a double envelopment and his party sustained a number of casualties. Laurens was killed at the first fire. The British captured the howitzer.

A second engagement began when Gen. Gist arrived sometime later, but the American commander soon called off the attack when it became apparent that the Patriot cavalry had insufficient room to maneuver. The British were also going to make effective use of the captured howitzer. Brereton's troops traveled a short distance downstream, boarded their ships, and departed from Fields Point.

Date visited: _____

Comments: _____

_____

_____

Lowcountry
Region 4 Site 60

Port Royal Island*

1 February 2–3, 1779

2 July 8–15, 1779

32.47885°N 80.73715°W

Beaufort County

Result: Patriot victory

Combatants	
Great Britain	United States Patriot militia
Commanders and Leaders	
Gen. Augustine Prévost	Brig. Gen. William Moultrie
Strength	
Approx. 450	300
Casualties and Losses	
40 killed and wounded 7 captured	8 killed 22 wounded 300 slaves captured

Port Royal Island #1: February 2–3, 1779: To establish an initial British foothold in South Carolina, British Gen. Augustine Prévost sent a detachment from Savannah under the command of Maj. Valentine Gardiner to occupy Port Royal Island. His landing was on February 2 at Loyalist Andrew DeVeaux's plantation. The British attacked Patriot militia guarding South Carolina Patriot militia Gen. Stephen Bull's plantation next door to DeVeaux's plantation and burned Bull's house. The next day, the British first marched north to the Port Royal Ferry to prevent American forces from getting onto the Island, but learned that Patriot troops were already on the Island. The British then turned around and marched south towards Beaufort to engage the Patriots. American Gen. William Moultrie marched north from Beaufort with 300 militia, many of whom were from Gen. Stephen Bull's Beaufort area militia, to fight Gardiner. The battle took place at the swamp a few miles north of Beaufort and north of the Halfway House at Gray's Hill. This is one of the rare actions where the British had the cover of the trees and the Patriots were in the open field and where the militia did stand and fight instead of running from British regulars. The Americans, under Moultrie's command, defeated the British and drove them from Port Royal Island. This action denied the British their much-desired foothold in South Carolina, for the moment.

Result: Patriot victory

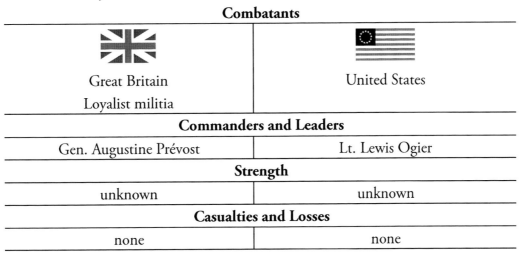

Combatants	
Great Britain Loyalist militia	United States
Commanders and Leaders	
Gen. Augustine Prévost	Lt. Lewis Ogier
Strength	
unknown	unknown
Casualties and Losses	
none	none

Port Royal Island #2: July 8–15, 1779: After the Battle of Stono Ferry in southern Charleston County, the British, commanded by British Gen. Augustine Prévost, left Edisto Island to withdraw towards Savannah, Georgia, moving south by island hopping down the South Carolina coast, crossing the bays by boat. They arrived at St. Helena Island and split their force between St. Helena and Ladies Islands. Crossing the Beaufort River on July 8th, 1779, they were able to occupy Beaufort without any resistance from the Americans. The Americans watched the British from Sheldon Church and harassed them at Beaufort and on the sea islands. The Americans skirmished in the Beaufort area in mid-July 1779 when American Lt. Lewis Ogier attacked a group of Loyalists driving about 300 head of cattle to feed Prévost's army. Ogier captured the battle and drove the Loyalists into the river. There were no reported casualties on either side. The precise location of this action is unknown, but happened close to Beaufort on Port Royal Island.

*Marker
Battle of Port Royal Island

Near the old halfway house, in the vicinity of Grays Hill, on February 3, 1779, a force of South Carolina Militia, Continentals, and volunteers, including men from Beaufort, under General William Moultrie, defeated the British in their attempt to capture Port Royal Island.

Erected: by Beaufort County Historical Society.

Date visited: _____

Comments: _____

_____

_____

Lowcountry
Region 4 Site 61

Battle of Coosawhatchie Bridge*

32.58843°N 80.92686°W

May 3, 1779

Jasper County

Result: Draw

Combatants	
Great Britain	United States Patriot militia
Commanders and Leaders	
Gen. Augustine Prévost	Lt. Col. John Laurens
Strength	
Approx. 1,000	Approx. 600
Casualties and Losses	
unknown	3 killed 8 wounded

American Southern Department commander Gen. Benjamin Lincoln decided to move against the British stronghold of Augusta, Georgia, with most of his army. British Gen. Augustine Prévost, at Savannah, learned of this plan, crossed the Savannah River with the greater part of his army and advanced overland to threaten Charleston. Gen. William Moultrie, who commanded two Continental regiments, opposed the British advance into South Carolina but Prévost's army outnumbered him. Moultrie, carefully choosing grounds to the Patriots' advantage, determined to stand for battle at Tullifinny Hill just east of the Tullifinny River. Lt. Col. John Laurens, son of the President of Congress, Henry Laurens, with 250 North Carolina Light Infantry and 150 picked riflemen, was detached to act as the rear guard. Laurens was ordered by Moultrie to withdraw the troops that were deployed to cover other Coosawhatchie River crossings and Moultrie's flanks and join the main army at the hill just to the east of Tullifinny river where Moultrie had deployed his troops. These light infantry, riflemen, and rear guard composed almost one-fourth of Moultrie's army. Instead of following orders and withdrawing the rear guard to Moultrie's chosen defensive position, Col. Laurens concentrated these men on the east side of the Coosawhatchie River, posted the riflemen at the bridge, threw off the bridge planks, and stopped to engage the British advance troops. The British, equipped with artillery, occupied the houses on the west bank of the Coosawhatchie River for cover from which they kept up a heavy and well-directed fire. A number of Laurens' men were killed and wounded. Laurens, conspicuous on horseback in a regimental uniform with a large white plume in his hat, was wounded and his horse killed. Laurens ordered Capt. Thomas Shubrick to hold this position and was withdrawn for medical care; then Shubrick wisely ordered the Patriots to retreat. Meanwhile, faced with the loss of the concentration of his forces, Moultrie decamped and started to withdraw his now demoralized army toward Charleston. Lauren's troops followed, but had to pass the Tullifinny and Pocotaligo bridges on the stringers, as the bridges' cross planks had been thrown off to delay the British advance. Lauren's troops did not overtake the main body of the American army until they had crossed Saltketcher Bridge. Laurens, without artillery or sufficient force, on disadvantaged ground, engaged the British without orders and did not burn down the houses west of the river. A retreat to the defenses of the City of Charleston was Moultrie's only practical course of action, leaving coastal South Carolina open for Prévost's unopposed advance. Prévost's march to Charleston was characterized by arson, plunder, and destruction.

*Marker
Coosawhatchie, dating to the 1740s, was named for the Coosaw Tribe. At first it was little more than a store and inn built on the King's Highway by Henry De Saussure, a Huguenot settler from Purrysburg. By the 1760s, it was a regional trading post and crossroads. During the Revolution British troops burned most of the buildings and the nearby bridge in a 1779 raid.

Coosawatchie served as the capital of Beaufort District from 1789 to 1836, when a new courthouse was built in Gillisonville. In 1861–62 Gen. Robert E. Lee, commanding the Confederate Dept. of S.C. and Ga., had his headquarters here. In 1864, during the last months of the Civil War, several skirmishes were fought nearby. This has been a village of farmers and merchants ever since.
Battle of Coosawhatchie

Coosawhatchie
Jasper County, South Carolina
Commanders: Colonels William Moultrie, John Laurens; Gen. Augustine Prevost
Casualties: 3 Americans killed, 8 wounded
"Despite the defeat at Port Royal Island, General Prevost was determined to make a second attempt to capture Charleston. Instead of a small detachment of 150 men, this time he crossed the Savannah River with 2,400 British regulars, and once again, William Moultrie

was outnumbered 2 to 1. He determined to make a stand on a slight ridge at the Tullifinny River, about 2 miles east of the Coosawhatchie River, where he left about 200 men to guard the crossing and warn him of the Redcoats arrival. As the enemy drew near,

Moultrie was about to send an aide to pull these troops back to the main force when Col. John Laurens offered to lead them back. Moultrie had so much confidence in the officer that he sent along 250 men to help cover the flanks, In direct disobedience of orders Laurens crossed the river and formed the men in line for battle. He failed to take the high ground and his men suffered greatly from well-placed enemy fire. Laurens himself was wounded, and his second in command fell back to the main force at the Tullifinny, where Moultrie was compelled to retreat towards Charleston." Excerpt from South Carolina's Revolutionary War Battlefields A Tour Guide

Erected: by The South Carolina Historical Society.

Date visited: _____

Comments: _____

_____

_____

Lowcountry
Region 4 Site 62

Site of Purrysburg

April 29, 1779

32.29715°N 81.11942°W

Jasper County

Result: Unknown

Combatants	
Great Britain	United States
Commanders and Leaders	
Brig. Gen. Augustine Prevost	Maj. Gen. Benjamin Lincoln
Strength	
unknown	unknown
Casualties and Losses	
unknown	unknown

Purrysburg was the first headquarters of the Southern Continental Army within South Carolina under Major General Benjamin Lincoln. On April 29, 1779 British Brigadier General Augustine Prevost of Savannah, Georgia crossed the Savannah River to begin his march towards Charlestown in hopes of capturing it. On this date, a brief skirmish occurred between Maj. Gen. Lincoln's Continentals and Prevost's Loyalists near Purrysburg.

Date visited: _____

Comments: _____
_____
_____

**Lowcountry
Region 4 Site 63**

Battle at Eutaw Springs*

September 8, 1781

33.40735°N 80.29858°W

Orangeburg County

Result: Draw

Combatants	
Great Britain	United States
Loyalist militia	Patriot militia
Commanders and Leaders	
Lt. Col. Alexander Stewart	Maj. Gen. Nathanael Greene
Strength	
1,396	2,080
Casualties and Losses	
85 killed	251 killed
351 wounded	367 wounded
430 captured	unknown captured

Within four months after Gen. Nathanael Greene's return to South Carolina, his Southern Continental Army, together with South Carolina, North Carolina, and Virginia state troops and militia, broke the British hold on the interior by eliminating the Crown's posts one by one. American mounted detachments achieved a major psychological victory over the British by carrying the war almost to the gates of Charleston. A decisive blow was dealt to the British on the battlefield of Eutaw Springs.

The American commanders who took part in the famous Battle of Eutaw Springs, according to their positions in Greene's line of battle: The first line was composed of militia; on the right was the South Carolina militia of Gen. Francis Marion; on the left the South Carolina militia of Gen. Andrew Pickens; and in the center a French ally, the Col. Marquis de Malmedy, commanding the North Carolina militia. The left of this line was covered by the South Carolina state troops, under Lt. Col. William Henderson. The right flank was guarded by the legion of Lt. Col Henry Lee.

The second line was composed of the Continental troops. On the right were the North Carolina Continentals under Gen. Jethro Sumner, on the left were the Maryland Continentals under Col. Otho H. Williams, and in the center were the Virginia Continentals under Lt. Col. Richard Campbell. As usual, the American reserve was the cavalry of Lt. Col. William Washington.

Both the North and South Carolina militias and Continentals showed exemplary courage and discipline during this engagement. The British army was driven back one mile and through their camp, and Greene almost won one of the most spectacular American victories of the war. However, two factors prevented him from achieving a win. The first was due to the Americans getting tangled up in the British camp as the enemy retreated beyond it into range of the British soldiers strongly posted in a brick house. The second came from three determined British officers. Maj. John Marjoribanks anchored the British line and resisted the American advance from a thicket on the American left. Maj. John Coffin and his cavalry made a stiff resistance on the American right and Maj. Henry Sheridan rallied the retreating British at the strong brick house near the spring. He provided the basis of the British defense and counterattack.

After five hours of hard fighting in the Carolina summer heat, Greene withdrew from the British camp, leaving the British army still in its possession. Eutaw Springs was essentially a draw in which both sides claimed victory. In the view of history, however, the battle was both a material and moral victory for the Americans. The British had suffered such heavy losses that they could no longer exert control over South Carolina beyond Charleston and its immediate environs. This was the last major battle of the Revolution in South Carolina. The British troops at Eutaw Springs were to reinforce Lord Cornwallis at Yorktown, but because of their heavy losses in this battle, they retreated to Moncks Corner and to White's Meeting House (Dorchester County) to recover and rest. This battle aided the Americans at Yorktown in defeating Cornwallis.

*Marker
Victory in Defeat

On the morning of September 8, 1781, General Nathanael Greene's American army attacked Colonel Alexander Stewart's British Force camped at a plantation near Eutaw Springs. Here two almost evenly matched armies slugged it out in the last major Revolutionary War battle in South Carolina.

In over three hours of brutal combat, American and British forces traded musket volleys and bayonet charges. Greene's troops drove the British back into their camp, but the British regrouped and forced Greene from the battlefield.

The Americans suffered more than 500 casualties, but the British lost nearly 700. Crippled by the loss of almost a third of his command, Stewart retreated toward Charleston the following day, leaving most of the South Carolina countryside in American control.

A Close and Deadly Clash of Veteran Troops

Greene's army at Eutaw Springs consisted of regular soldiers and militia, or part-time citizen soldiers. Stewart's force was composed of British regulars and Loyalists, Americans fighting to preserve British rule. Each army mustered about 2000 men, most of them veterans.

Infantry—foot soldiers carrying single-shot, muzzle loading—muskets formed the bulk of both forces. Maneuvering in close ranks, they fired their muskets in short-ranged volleys and then charged with bayonets. Several small cannons supported both armies in the front lines. Small reserves of cavalry forces waited to exploit breakthroughs or cover retreats. While mounted, the cavalrymen fought mostly with heavy sabers. These tactics and weapons ensured that the opposing forces at Eutaw Springs would clash at close, deadly range.

Battle of Eutaw Springs
A Critical Loss of Discipline

" The rich prize within our grasp was lost"
          —Colonel Henry Lee

Late in the battle, American soldiers pushed forward and found themselves in the British camp. Victory was in sight, but the discipline that had held the American ranks together through the hours of hard fighting broke down when the ragged soldiers stopped to loot British tents.

Loyalist troops barricaded in the two-story brick plantation house nearby poured musket fire into the Americans below. As the American advance stalled in front of this strongpoint, the British counterattacked and drove the Americans back out of their camp. His soldiers exhausted and low on ammunition, Greene retreated, leaving the bloody field in Stewart's hands.

To Major Marjoribanks and the flank battalion under his command " I think the honour of the day is due."

—Colonel Alexander Stewart

Major John Marjoribanks (pronounced "Marshbanks") led a battalion of elete troops that held the right flank of Stewart's British army. From a dense oak thicket, Marjoribanks' men held their position against repeated attacks until they were driven back to a palisade fence around the plantation house. From there they continued to inflict heavy casualties on the attacking Americans. When the Americans halted their charge to loot the British camp, Marjoribanks led his battalion in a counterattack that helped turn the tide of battle. But the veteran officer had little chance to savor the victory—he died a month later.

Battle of Eutaw
This stone marks the field whereon was fought the battle of Eutaw, September 8, 1781, between a force of the United States under Major General Nathanael Greene and a force of Great Britain under Colonel Stuart. Neither side was victorious, but the fight was beneficial to the American Cause.
Erected by Eutaw Chapter D.A.R. 1912

(Lower Plaque)
This Memorial erected in 1912 by Eutaw Chapter NSDAR
Orangeburg, S.C.

Erected: 1912 by Eutaw Chapter NSDAR Orangeburg, S.C.

Date visited: _____

Comments: _____

_____

_____

Siege of Fort Motte

33.76053°N 80.66978°W

May 8–12, 1781

Calhoun County

Result: Patriot victory

Combatants	
Great Britain	United States Patriot militia
Commanders and Leaders	
Lt. Donald McPherson	Brig. Gen. Francis Marion
Strength	
184	450
Casualties and Losses	
183 captured	none

This British garrison, commanded by Lt. Donald McPherson, took over the mansion house belonging to Mrs. Rebecca Motte. Opposite the garrison, to the north, stood another hill where Mrs. Motte now resided in a farmhouse. At this height, South Carolina Patriot Lt. Col. Henry Lee posted his troops, while South Carolina Brig. Gen. Francis Marion occupied the eastern portion of the ridge. Since British Lord Rawdon had camped within a 48-hour march, time was of the essence and Mrs. Motte was informed that the Americans intended to set fire to her mansion to dislodge the British. She declared she would be happy to help the Patriot cause this way. This was not accomplished with burning arrows, as many believe, but by a ball of sulfur and rosin made by Nathan Savage. This was slung onto the roof, after the roof had time to dry from the morning dew. The British tried to remove the burning shingles, but failed due to Patriot cannon fire and soon evacuated the house. On the British surrender, Gen. Marion's men extinguished the fire.

Date visited: _____

Comments: _____

_____

_____

Fun Facts

When was the 18th century?

The 18th Century began on January 1, 1700 and lasted through December 31, 1799. We are currently in the 21st century and will be so until January 1, 2100.

What is hallowed ground?

Hallowed ground refers to a parcel of land or place of reverence and remembrance to an event or where many people are buried. A cemetery is hallowed ground just as a battlefield is hallowed ground, due to the blood spilled there.

What is a meeting house?

A Meeting House in the 18th century was built using tax money and was the focal point for the community where the town's residents could discuss local issues, conduct religious worship, and engage in town business.

When did Carolina split into North Carolina and South Carolina?

Due to diverging cultures/ personalities and the two major cities being so far apart, in 1712 the colonists in New Bath, North Carolina petitioned the King of England to become a separate colony from the colonists centered around Charles Town, South Carolina.

What were the 7 districts in SC during the Rev War?

This book has the state divided into 4 regions with 46 counties. But the original districts are listed below: (There were no counties during the American Revolution.)

- Beaufort
- Camden
- Charleston
- Cheraw
- Georgetown
- Ninety Six
- Orangeburg

Is there a Long Island, South Carolina?

Yes, the island is 7 miles long and 1 mile wide and has been renamed the Isle of Palms.

Why does South Carolina have names such as: Charles Town (Charleston), Georgetown, Kingstree…?

Streets, towns and cities in the colonies were given names that either honored the British crown, or were named after the place in England where the colonists emigrated from.

Why is water so important to the 18th century?

Water held and still holds a significant importance to people both now and in the 18th century. Clean water for drinking is important to basic survival, water is how goods were transported not only across oceans but throughout the colonies on rivers and lakes as well. Water travel was faster than land in the 18th century and connected people in ways that dangerous country roads could not. Sometimes water was used as a natural barrier to stop the enemy from advancing in battle. Not only does water keep one alive, but is a versatile part of the landscape that helped shape how this country developed.

What were the most prevalent diseases in South Carolina during the 1700s?

Smallpox and malaria were two diseases that ran rampant throughout the colonies in the 1700s. Malaria could be treated with quinine though and if inoculated, one could be protected from smallpox.

What animals were in South Carolina that caused the British problems?

—Marsh Tacky Horses (South Carolina's state horse)

—Alligators

—No Seeums (these are tiny insects that bite multiple times and the bites are very uncomfortable.)

—Rattlesnakes, which are only found in North America

—Wild boars and hogs

Is salt really that important in the 18th century and the American Revolution?

Yes, it has been used for food preservation and seasoning for thousands of years. Most importantly, salt helped eliminate the dependence on seasonal availability of food, and made it possible to transport food over large distances.

Why were pine trees so important to the 18th century?

Pine trees grow tall and straight and were used to build the ship's mast. Ships were the only way to transport goods across the ocean during the 18th century, so it was very important to have a strong and fast ship. Tar from the pine tree was also used to waterproof and seal ships and barrels of goods.

What is tabby?

Tabby is a type of concrete made by burning oyster shells to create lime, then mixing it with water, sand, ash and broken oyster shells. Tabby was used by colonists primarily in coastal South Carolina and Georgia.

What were the cash crops in South Carolina in the 18th century?

Rice and Indigo

What was a major trade item in South Carolina in the 18th century?

Deerskins

What is so special about sweetgrass baskets?

Sweetgrass baskets are unique to South Carolina and the Gullah culture, one thing that makes sweetgrass baskets special is that they aren't made with typical weaving techniques like plaiting or twisting, which are common in other parts of the world. Instead, Gullah artists employ the West African tradition of coiling. Dried sweetgrass is bundled together and coiled in circles.

What were the bare minimum requirements to become a soldier in the Continental Army?

Besides being of legal age, a man had to have at least two teeth, top and bottom to rip open paper with gun powder in it.

How much territory did the British control during the American Revolution?

Throughout the American Revolution the British controlled a number of key cities throughout the colonies, New York, Savannah, Charlestown, and temporarily they also controlled Boston and Philadelphia. However, about 90% of American colonists did not live in the cities, but rather in the rural countryside outside of British control. So, while the British controlled the ports for supplies and news, they never really had control over the people throughout the American Revolution.

Which battles had the greatest number of soldiers fighting in it?

1.	Battle of Long Island, NY	1776	40,000 men fighting
2.	Brandywine, PA	1777	30,000 men fighting
3.	Yorktown, VA	1781	27,000 men fighting

Which battle did the Americans lose the most men in?

When Charleston fell to the British in 1780 the Continental army lost 5,000 soldiers as prisoners of war. At the battle of Long Island, NY in 1776, the Americans had around 2,000 men killed, wounded, or captured.

Which battle did the British lose the most men in?

After the battle of Yorktown in VA, the British surrendered over 8,000 soldiers. However, at both Cowpens and Kings Mountain in SC the British lost about 90% of the armies as prisoners of war, so while the number of men lost was smaller, a greater impact was felt at both of those battles compared to Yorktown.

What was the mostly costly battle during the Rev War?

The crushing defeat of the Continental Army at the battle of Camden, S.C. stands out as the most costly battle of the war. Approximately 1,050 continental troops were killed and wounded, while the British suffered 314 casualties.

What happened on June 28, 1776?

On this day Colonel William Moultrie and about 400 continental soldiers successfully defended against the British invading forces in an incomplete fort on Sullivan's Island. It is now called Carolina Day and commemorates the small Patriot force defeating the large British Navy.

Where was Moultrie's flag first flown in South Carolina?

General William Moultrie's flag was first flown at Fort Johnson.

What happened on December 14, 1782?

Also known as Victory Day, on this day the British completely evacuated from Charleston and South Carolina. Thus as General William Moultrie is credited with saying, "This fourteenth day of December, 1782, ought never to be forgotten by the Carolinians; it ought to be the day of festivity with them, as it is the real day of their deliverance and independence."

Who was the prisoner exchanged for Lord Conrwallis and held in the Tower of London in 1781?

Henry Laurens, father of John Laurens.

By the Numbers

Below are the statistics for each of the main fighting forces. Due to inaccurate data kept at the time, all numbers shown below are experts best guesses.

	American	British	Hessians	French
Regular Army	231,000	22,000	30,000	12,000
Militia	145,000	25,000		
Total	376,000	47,000	30,000	12,000
Killed	6,800		1,200	
Wounded	6,100			
Disease	17,000		6,354	
Total	29,900	24,000	7,554	

*During and after the American Revolutionary War approximately 5,500 Hessians deserted and settled down in America, instead of going back home to what is now known as Germany.

Children

Children during the American Revolutionary War helped out the war cause in various ways. Boys ages 16 and up could join the military and fought on either side of the war. Those who were too young to fight worked for the military as musicians, messengers, or handing powder to the men loading the cannons. Young Andrew Jackson, who would one day become America's seventh president, joined the military at the age of 13. Some young women hid their identities and fought in the war as well, Deborah Sampson is one such example. All children helped out in the war effort by growing food, sewing uniforms, and tending to wounded soldiers. With parents away fighting, the older children also took on the responsibility of keeping the homefront going for when their parents would hopefully return from fighting.

Women

Women took on multiple roles during the American Revolution, just as they continue to do today.

Some women became camp followers and served as washerwomen, cooks, nurses, supply scavengers, seamstresses, and some fought or worked as spies. Emily Geiger volunteered to ride 70 miles through dangerous backcountry to deliver a message to Gen. Thomas Sumter from Gen. Nathanael Greene. While trying to reach Gen. Sumter, Emily was captured by the British for being a suspected spy. Before being taken to Lord Rawdon, Emily quickly memorized the message and ate the parchment before the British could find it. Once released from the British, Emily quickly continued on her way to Gen. Sumter to deliver the message. Due to Emily's quick thinking and excellent memory, Gen. Sumter was able to ride to Gen. Greene's aide within an hour. Another example is Kate Barry, who warned her neighbors of the British advance prior to the Battle of Cowpens.

It was women at home that led the boycott of British goods after the Tea Act and Boston Tea Party of 1773, also known as the Homespun Movement. Wives of high ranking generals would at times visit the men at camp and spend time with the sick and wounded, for example Martha Washington and Kitty Greene. Their presence in camp might not have helped move the battle lines forward, but it did boost the mens' morale and reminded them about what they were fighting for. Some women even gave over their homes for the war effort, housing and feeding soldiers from both sides at different times, like Mary Dilliard prior to the Battle of Blackstock Plantation. Rebecca Motte from South Carolina made the ultimate sacrifice and allowed Francis Marion to burn her home down to get rid of the British. Women fought both from their homes and in the camps, sacrificing for the cause as much as the soldiers fighting in the battles and skirmishes throughout the colonies. Though many women helped during the war for our independence through faith, courage and intelligence; many of their names have been lost in history due to the fact that men were the primary authors of our history books.

Great Seal of South Carolina

The Great Seal of the State of South Carolina was adopted in 1776. South Carolina's seal is made up of two elliptical areas, linked by branches of the palmetto tree. The image on the left is dominated by a tall palmetto tree and an oak tree, fallen and broken. This scene represents the battle fought on June 28, 1776, between defenders of the unfinished fort on Sullivan's Island, and the British Fleet. The standing palmetto represents the victorious defenders, and the fallen oak is the British Fleet. Banded together on the palmetto with the motto *Quis separabit?* ('Who will separate?'), are 12 spears that represent the other original 12 states of the Union. Beneath that is enscrolled another of the alternate state mottos, "Meliorem Lapsa Locavit" ("Having Fallen, She Has Set Up a Better One") with the date of 1776. Surrounding the image, at the top, is "South Carolina", and below, is *Animis opibusque parati* ('Prepared in mind and resources'). The other image on the seal depicts the Roman goddess, Spes walking along a shore that is littered with weapons. The goddess grasps a branch of laurel as the sun rises behind her. Below her image is her name, *Spes*, Latin for 'hope', and over the image is the motto *Dum spiro spero*, meaning 'While I breathe, I hope'.

Capital Cities of South Carolina & Their Names

In 1670 the colony of Carolina was established and its capital was Charles Town, soon changed to "Charlestown." Charlestown was named in honor of King Charles I of England. After the British seized Charlestown in 1780 the provincial state capital of South Carolina was temporarily moved further inland to Jacksonboro, SC. (More detail given in Region 4 Site 57). At the end of the American Revolution in 1783, Charlestown was once again the state capital. The new state of South Carolina wanted to further separate their identity from the British Empire and "americanized" the city's name to a shortened name of "Charleston," which has been used ever since.

The capital of South Carolina was moved in 1786 as a compromise between the Backcountry farmers and the Lowcountry plantation owners. The Backcountry wanted a more centrally located capital to air grievances and make laws. The Lowcountry wanted a safer capital, that was not so easily taken in any future invasions of hostile forces. Thus Columbia was founded and made the state capital of South Carolina in 1786. Senator John Lewis Gervais introduced the bill to move the state capital and gave an impassioned speech stating, "In this town we should find refuge under the wings of COLUMBIA." leading to the capital being named after America's goddess of liberty instead of naming it "Washington," after our first president. Columbia beat out Washington in an 11-7 vote in the state senate.

There is a misinterpretation that has been spread since the naming of the first planned state capital. Many have come to believe that Columbia was Christopher Colombus' name feminized and meant to represent America's sense of exploration and new lands of opportunity. While the name "Columbia" was initially derived from Christopher Columbus in 1697, by 1760 Columbia had come to be the embodiment of liberty and a New World goddess throughout Europe and the American Colonies. This idea of Columbia as a goddess of liberty can be seen in a book of poems printed from Harvard University in 1761. However, it was Phillis Wheatley's poem to George Washington in 1775 that solidified Columbia as the goddess representing America and liberty.

As previously stated, Columbia was a planned city. When it came to naming the streets of the city a lot of thought was placed on how to properly honor not only the state of South Carolina, but the people who made the state and new capital possible. All the streets that run north to south in Columbia were originally named after general officers that served in South Carolina during the Revolutionary War. The parallel streets east of Assembly Street from the State House are named in honor of the militia officers of South Carolina; for example, Sumter, Marion, Bull, and Pickens. The parallel streets west of Assembly Street from the State House are named in honor of the Continental army generals who served in South Carolina; for example, Gates, Lincoln, Gadsden, and Huger. All the streets that run west to east in Columbia were originally named to honor the people who made Columbia as a city possible and the major industries that propelled South Carolina forward. The parallel streets that run south of Senate Street from the State House are named after crops and products important to South Carolina; for example, Blossom (as in, cotton blossom), Wheat, Tobacco, and Indigo (which was made into a major cash crop in the 1700's by botanist and businesswoman, Eliza Pinckney). The parallel streets that run north of Senate Street from the State House are named after contemporary individuals who made the city of Columbia and South Carolina a reality; for example, Gervais, Washington (after George Washington), Lady (after Lady Martha Washington), Taylor (The man whose land was absorbed to make Columbia into a city.), and Plain (The track of land absorbed to build the city.)

The Evolution of Camden

To trace the various names for the city of Camden, South Carolina is a difficult task. Camden has been burned down several times since being "officially" settled in 1732, and each fire takes with it not only buildings and livelihoods, but decades worth of historical town records as well. What is left of the records is not a complete picture and is at times hard to distinguish town lines and times of occupation in the area. From what has been gathered and passed along in the historical record, the area of Camden was once the principal seat to the kingdom of Cofitachequi which was occupying the area around the 1300's until it was "abandoned" by 1701. In 1732 the township of Fredericksburg was established, though unsettled by European colonists at the time. Around 1757 Quakers settled in the area and began friendly relations with the Catawba, calling their settlement "Pine Tree Hill," while the general area was still referred to as Fredericksburg. Joseph Kershaw was granted 250 acres of land in 1765, which was located in the northern area of present day Camden. Kershaw called his budding town, "Log Town." Charles Pratt, Lord Camden in England was an advocate of the American colonists' rights and was therefore honored with the renaming of "Pine Tree Hill" to "Camden" on April 12, 1768. Thus Camden and Log Town made up what is now present day Camden. Camden continued to grow and on December 24, 1890 was officially declared a city.

Gadsden and His Flag

Christopher Gadsden was born in Charleston South Carolina in 1724 and raised to become a wealthy Charleston merchant. In 1765 Gadsden led the Sons of Liberty in South Carolina and later was often called, "the Sam Adams of the South." In 1775 he was chosen to represent South Carolina at the Continental Congress in Philadelphia and was one of three members of the Marine Committee.

A close friend of Benjamin Franklin, Gadsden took inspiration from the political cartoon Franklin had created during the French and Indian War about a rattlesnake being chopped up, telling people to "Join or Die." While designing the flag for the first Commander-in-Chief of the United States

Navy, Esek Hopkins; Gadsden used the rattlesnake on a field of yellow, warning the enemy, "Do Not Tread On Me." According to notes by Franklin the rattlesnake is an excellent representation for the American spirit due to multiple factors. One, the rattlesnake is only found in the Americas. Two, the rattlesnake never begins a fight, but once engaged, never surrenders. And lastly, the rattlesnake has sharp eyes and "may therefore be esteemed an emblem of vigilance." Gadsden presented his flag to the Provincial Congress in South Carolina in February of 1776. It should be noted that there are thirteen rattles on the snake's tail, each rattle meant to represent a colony and that without everyone working together, America would not be a threat to the British.

Gadsden's flag was first seen in use during the Navy's first engagement in 1775 to capture arms and gunpowder from British ships. The Marines on board the ship had painted their drums yellow and placed the rattlesnake upon them with the "Do Not Tread on Me" motto. The Navy and marines went on to achieve many crucial victories throughout the war and the Gadsden flag is still used to this day.

William Jasper and His Flags

Not much is known about William Jasper other than he came from South Carolina and was born around 1750. On June 28th, 1776, an approximately 16 year old William Jasper was a sergeant in the 2nd South Carolina Regiment, stationed at the incomplete Fort Sullivan in Charlestown, SC. While the British Navy bombarded the incomplete fort, the flag staff with South Carolina's flag was shot down. Risking life and limb, William Jasper traversed the fort to raise the flag once again over the fort, holding the flag up under fire until another flagstaff could be raised. Jasper was given the personal sword of South Carolina Governor John Rutledge by the governor after the battle in recognition of his bravery.

Three years later William Jasper was serving under General Benjamin Lincoln when they attempted to recapture the city of Savannah from the British. On October 9, 1779, the 24th day of the siege to try and recapture Savannah, William Jasper again risked his life to rescue one of his regiment's flags. Unfortunately this young man's life was cut short when he received a mortal wound during the attempt and died during the battle. William Jasper left behind a widow and at least two children, but he was memorialized in South Carolina and Georgia for his bravery and courage under fire, and the determination to keep his flags flying during the fight for independence and liberty.

Significant Leaders and Heroes of the Revolutionary War

British:

General Sir Henry Clinton (April 16, 1730–December 23, 1795) was a British army officer and politician, best known for his service as a general during the American War of Independence. First arriving in Boston in May 1775, from 1778 to 1782, he was the British Commander-in-Chief in North America.

Lord Charles Cornwallis (December 31, 1738–October 5, 1805) was with the British army during the occupation of South Carolina. He was ordered to suppress the resistance efforts of Francis Marion and Thomas Sumter. He failed to do so and brought his weakened army to North Carolina, then to his ultimate surrender at Yorktown.

Lord Francis Rawdon (December 9, 1754–November 28, 1826) following the Siege of Charleston, Lord Cornwallis assigned Lord Rawdon to command the advance post at Camden. He played an active role in the Southern Campaign. When Cornwallis advanced north after Cowpens, Rawdon was left to defend South Carolina and Georgia.

Colonel Alexander Stewart (c. 1739–December 16, 1794) was a Scottish officer in the British Army. In the summer of 1781, he became commander of British troops in Charleston. After the fall of British outposts at Augusta and Ninety Six, Stewart led a 2,000 man army inland to meet the threat of Nathanael Greene advancing on Charleston. The two armies met at the Battle of Eutaw Springs in September, 1781, where Stewart was wounded.

Sir Banastre Tarleton (August 21, 1754–January 15, 1833) was the British lieutenant colonel and commander of the British Legion. He was infamous for his ruthless cruelty and treatment of those sympathetic with the Patriot cause.

American:

<u>Baron de Kalb</u> (June 19, 1721–August 19, 1780) was a Bavarian-French military officer who served as a major general in the Continental Army during the American Revolutionary War and was mortally wounded in action while fighting the British Army during the Battle of Camden.

<u>General Horatio Gates</u> (July 26, 1727–April 10, 1806) was an English-born American general in the American Revolution. Commander at the Battle of Camden.

<u>Colonel William "Danger" Thomson</u> (July 5, 1736–September 3, 1781) was responsible for defeating the British land assault on Sullivan's Island at Breach Inlet and was one of South Carolina's outstanding citizen-soldiers of the American Revolution.

<u>General Thomas Sumter</u> (August 14, 1734–June 1, 1832) was a soldier in the Colony of Virginia militia; brigadier general in the South Carolina militia during the American Revolution, a planter, and a politician.

<u>General Francis Marion</u> (c.1732–February 27, 1795) was a native of the Cooper River region. He used his unmatched knowledge of the Lowcountry to conduct guerilla raids against the British and Loyalist outposts throughout baronies surrounding Charleston and then retreated to the safety of the swamps and forest. His elusiveness earned him the nickname "the Swamp Fox."

<u>General Andrew Pickens</u> (September 13, 1739–August 11, 1817) was the son of Scots-Irish immigrants. He rose to the rank of brigadier general during the Cherokee War. During the Siege of Charleston, Pickens surrendered to the British under the terms that he sit out the war and they would leave him alone. When the British violated those terms by destroying the majority of his property, Pickens took up arms against them and joined Sumter and Marion as a leader of partisan forces.

<u>Brigadier General William Washington</u> (February 28, 1752–March 6, 1810) was George Washington's second cousin. He was a talented commander of light dragoons in the SOuthern Campaign. Rising in rank to lieutenant colonel, one of his notable successes was the capture of Rugeley's Mill using a "Quaker gun."

<u>Brigadier General William Moultrie</u> (November 23, 1730–September 27, 1805) his defense of Sullivan's Island was the first significant Patriot victory in the Revolutionary War and prevented the British from taking Charleston. The fort was later named in his honor. He led troops at the Siege of

Savannah, the Battle of Port Royal Island, and the Siege of Charleston. After serving two terms as Governor, he was the first president of South Carolina's Society of the Cincinnati chapter.

General Nathanael Greene (August 7, 1747–July 19, 1786) after the Battle of Camden, he succeeded Horatio Gates in his post as Commander of the Continental forces in South Carolina. He used his understanding of mobile warfare and the importance of partisan forces to secure South Carolina' s liberation.

Colonel Wade Hampton (c.1752–February 4, 1835) was a revered cavalry commander, leading Hampton's Regiment of Light Dragoons. He served both Lt. Col. William Washington and Brig. Gen. Thomas Sumter. He distinguished himself at the Battle of Eutaw Springs.

General Daniel Morgan (July 6, 1736–July 6, 1802) was a son of poor Welsh immigrants who rose to the rank of brigadier general. He was called to the Southern Theatre by Horatio Gates and remained there under Nathanael Greene. Morgan, the "Old Waggoner," was known for his exceptional use of military tactics. His plan at Cowpens is considered to be the tactical masterpiece of the war.

Sergeant William Jasper (c.1750–October 9, 1779) distinguished himself in the defense of Fort Sullivan, now called Fort Moultric. When a shell from a British warship shot down the flagstaff, he recovered the South Carolina flag, raised it on a temporary staff, and held it under fire until a new staff was installed. Later Governor John Rutledge gave his sword to Jasper in recognition of his bravery.

Lieutenant Daniel Gilbert (c.1732–c.1805) served in the French and Indian War and also in the American Revolution. My hero and fifth great grandfather. His father arrived in Baltimore, Maryland from England in 1695.

Henry Laurens (March 6, 1724–December 8, 1792) was an American statesman who served as president of the Continental Congress (1777–78). After pursuing a profitable career as a merchant and planter, Laurens espoused the patriot cause in the disputes with Great Britain preceding the American Revolution. He was made president of the South Carolina Council of Safety and vice president of the state in 1776. Sent as a delegate to the Continental Congress meeting at Philadelphia, he was soon elected chief officer of that body. In August 1780 Laurens embarked on a mission to Holland to negotiate on behalf of Congress a $10,000,000 loan, but he was captured off Newfoundland and imprisoned in the Tower of London. On Dec. 31, 1781, he was released on parole and finally exchanged for the British general Charles Cornwallis. He and his son, John are buried at Mepkin Abbey.

Benjamin Lincoln (January 24, 1733—May 9, 1810) was an American army officer. He served as a major general in the Continental Army during the American Revolutionary War. Lincoln was involved in three major surrenders during the war: his participation in the Battles of Saratoga (sustaining a wound shortly afterward) contributed to John Burgoyne's surrender of a British army, he oversaw the largest American surrender of the war at the 1780 Siege of Charleston, and, as George Washington's second in command, he formally accepted the British surrender at Yorktown.

Isaac Huger (March 19, 1743– October 17, 1797) was a planter and Continental Army general during the American Revolutionary War.

10 Recommended Sites to Definitely Visit

1. The Revolutionary War Visitor Center
2. Fort Moultrie/ Breach Inlet
3. Historic Camden
4. Eutaw Springs Battle Park/ Francis Marion's Grave
5. Musgrove Mill State Site
6. Historic Brattonsville
7. Cowpens Battlefield
8. Ninety Six Historic Site
9. Walnut Grove Plantation
10. Kings Mountain National Park

Additional Sites to Visit:

1. Ruins of Sheldon Church (aka Prince William's Parish): built 1753, burned by the British in 1779.
2. Old St. David's Church: The last Anglican or "state" church built c. 1770 under King George III. The church was used as a hospital during the Rev War. Members named their church for the Patron Saint of Wales to honor the native country of many Cheraw settlers.
3. South Carolina plantations that were present during the Revolutionary War.
4. Andrew Jackson State Park
5. Catawba Cultural Center
6. Charles Pinckney National Historic Site

7. Charleston Tea Plantation

8. Colonial Dorchester State Historic Site

9. Georgetown Harborwalk

10. Hampton Plantation State Historic Site

11. Historic Brattonsville

12. Hopsewee Plantation

13. I'on Swamp Interpretive Trail

14. Kings Mountain State Park

15. Living History Park in North Augusta

16. Middleton Place

17. Musgrove Mill State Historic State

18. Ninety Six National Historic Site

19. Boone Hall Plantation

Gravesites to Visit

1. William Davie: Old Presbyterian Church at Waxhaws

2. John & Henry Laurens: Mepkin Abbey

3. Francis Marion: Eutaw Springs

4. WIlliam Moultrie: Fort Moultrie (Formerly named Fort Sullivan)

5. Andrew Pickens: Oconee County

6. Thomas Sumter: High Hills of Santee

7. Baron Johann de Kalb: Old Presbyterian Church in Camden

8. Joseph Kershaw: Camden

9. Daniel Gilbert: near the Cowpens battlefield

10. There are several Revolutionary gravesites located at St. Michael's and St. Phillip's churches in Charleston.

Appendix

"Looking Back at *The Patriot*"
by Dr. Anthony J. Scotti, Jr.

On June 28, 2000, cinemas across the United States commenced showing *The Patriot,* a film of 2 hours and 45 minutes in duration, Directed by Roland Emmerich (who also has the big-budget *Independence Day, Godzilla,* and *The Day After Tomorrow* to his credit) and written by Robert Rodat (the same writer for *Saving Private Ryan*), this epic had a budget of $110 million and grossed more than $215 million worldwide. The production is truly a "South Carolina original" as it was filmed at a variety of locations in the state, including Historic Brattonsville, Charleston, Chester, Fort Lawn, Georgetown, Moncks Corner, Rock Hill, and York (the scenes of the lush countryside of York County are indeed quite recognizable.) The storyline is based loosely on the Southern campaigns of the Revolutionary War (1775–1783) and focuses on the activities of the partisan Francis Marion, i.e. the "Swamp Fox," and Banastre Tarleton, the leader of the feared and infamous British Legion."[1]

The public reception of the movie was mixed. Many living history enthusiasts were aghast immediately at the inaccurate uniforms, the use of siege artillery in several battlefield scenes, the density of linear formations, etc. In fact, International Movie Database (IMDb) lists some 132 "goofs," including twenty-two anachronisms, ten character flaws, and twenty-four factual errors.[2] Yet, an October 2020 *Journal of the American Revolution* article ranking American Revolution movies and television productions still assigned *The Patriot* a moderate designation of "6," right ahead of *April Morning* and right behind the AMC miniseries *TURN.*[3]

The distinguished University of South Carolina History professor Walter Edgar maintained that *The Patriot* captured "the feeling" of the events while actually downplaying British atrocities in the Southern theater. Alex von Tunzelmann, author of *Reel History: The World According to the*

1   "*The Patriot* (2000): Filming and Production," International Movie Database (IMDb), accessed January 29, 2022, https://www.imdb.com/title/tt0187393/?ref=fn_al_tt_1.

2   "*The Patriot* (2000): Goofs," IMDb, accessed January 29, 2022, https://www.imdb.com/title/tt0187393/goofs?tab=gf&ref_=tt_trv_gf.

3   John Knight, "Ranking American Revolution Films and Television," *Journal of the American Revolution,* October 6, 2020, https://allthingsliberty.com/author/john.

Movies (2017) stated: "Something historians have to contend with is that people have strong opinions and will try to assert them politically through film." Meanwhile director Spike Lee concluded that it is "blatant American Hollywood propaganda."[4]

Overall, there is much to bemoan and "call out" about *The Patriot*. Yet, what is more useful to historical inquiry is to identify the "telling moments" of the film. There are actually several key scenes in *The Patriot* that teach Americans much about their past and what they value as a people and nation.

The protagonist of *The Patriot* is Benjamin Martin (played by Mel Gibson), a character loosely based on Francis Marion but who is really a composite of not only that partisan leader but also Andrew Pickens, Thomas Sumter, and Daniel Morgan. Benjamin Martin is a complicated person, a man with great nobility of spirit and love of family while simultaneously possessing a furious nature and savage bent. Just like Francis Marion (c.1732–1795),[5] Martin served in the Cherokee expedition in 1761 and undoubtedly just like Marion, he is haunted by that experience, especially his misdeeds. The opening quote of the film reveals as much: "I have long feared that my sins would return to **v**isit me, and the cost is more than I can bear."[6] By today's standards, Martin is suffering from post-traumatic stress disorder or PTSD.

After the British army arrives in South Carolina in 1780, he earns the sobriquet the "Ghost" (in Marion's case, the "Swamp Fox") and with a handful of militia based deep in the swamps, they cause mayhem as the British attempt to subdue the colony. His base of operations in the film is a good depiction of Snow's Island, Marion's remote lair on the Pee Dee River, just east of present-day Johnsonville, South Carolina off U.S. Route 378. The site is currently a private hunting preserve, and even though it has been periodically logged over the years (the last time was 1955), it is essentially in an unaltered state. Marion operated here from December 1780 to March 1781, and a depression on the island appears to be the remains of his old earthworks."[7]

Martin is motivated to fight by revenge, not patriotism, and that is very interesting given the film's title. Initially, he is a neutral, at best a lukewarm patriot, since he knows very well what war

---

4   Tom Fordy, "Mel Gibson's War Atrocity: How *The Patriot* Whitewashed History and Demonised the British," *The Telegraph*, July 2, 2020, https://www.telegraph.co.uk.

5   Robert D. Bass, *Swamp Fox: The Life and Campaigns of General Francis Marion* (New York: Henry Holt, 1959).

6   *The Patriot,* directed by Roland Emmerich (Culver City, Calif.: Sony Pictures Home Entertainment, 2000), DVD.

7   "Snow's Island," South Carolina Preliminary Survey of Historic Places (1969), in South Carolina Department of Archives and History, Columbia, S.C.; Daniel W. Barefoot, *Touring South Carolina's Revolutionary War Sites* (Winston-Salem, N.C.: John F. Blair, 1999), 5–6.

entails. Plus, as a prosperous farmer and widower with a large family (seven children), and he has much to lose. In the South Carolina Commons House of Assembly, he expresses his fear of mob rule, i.e. mobocracy (for all its virtues, democracy was at one time equated with it!) When Martin finally decides to engage in the conflict, he proves to be a natural guerrilla leader, a formidable adversary worthy of his nickname "The Ghost." He knows not only where to acquire troops, but how to employ them and when to strike the enemy, thereby making an abject fool of the British commander in the South, Lord Cornwallis.

The antagonist Colonel William Tavington (played by Jason Isaacs), commander of the Green Dragoons, is more of a cut-and-dry character and is based on Banastre Tarleton (1754–1833).[8] Just like Tarleton, Tavington is the son of a mercantile family and is portrayed as a proverbial boogeyman, the very epitome of what the Americans were fighting against. (It can be argued that a Tarleton/Tavington figure shows up in every war!) His nature as a true English devil is revealed quite readily in two defining points in the film: the killing of wounded prisoners of war at the Martin homestead (a clear reference to the Battle of the Waxhaws in May 1780[9]) and the horrific moment that he orders civilians to be locked inside a church before the structure is burnt to the ground. With the second event, it should be noted that there is no such recorded incident occurring in the Revolutionary War and it is actually more reminiscent of Nazi atrocities in World War II (1939–1945). The film's German director reportedly told several reenactor extras on the set that since his nation got such bad press in the latter conflict, that it was high time the British got some too.[10] Even though that is clearly an overreach, such an abominable and demonic scene helped sell movie tickets! Be that as it may, the legacy of Tarleton and his British Legion redounded, as his second-in command Major George Hanger attested when he visited Princeton, New Jersey after the war and a local physician turned a deathly white when he discovered his true identity.[11]

The strategy employed in the Southern campaigns as well as the brutal civil war between Patriot (Whig) and Loyalist (Tory) are well captured in the film. The British commander in the Southern

---

8   Anthony J. Scotti, Jr., *Brutal Virtue: The Myth and Reality of Banastre Tarleton* (Bowie, Md.: Heritage, 2002).

9   Scotti, *Brutal Virtue*, 153–154n50, 173–178. For a good recent discussion of collective memory and mass violence, see Mark R. Anderson, *Down the Warpath to the Cedars: Indians' First Battles in the Revolution* (Norman: University of Oklahoma Press, 2021), 101.

10   The journalist Tom Fordy maintains that the British Empire lends itself to such an interpretation given that it was so large at one time and had oppressed so many people for so long. Fordy, "Mel Gibson's War Atrocity."

11   Scotti, *Brutal Virtue*, 31.

theater, Lieutenant General Charles, Earl Cornwallis (1738–1805) had no easy task in reasserting Crown rule but he was certainly no fool as portrayed on the screen. The real Cornwallis had a large swath of territory to control and long supply lines to protect with a limited number of troops. Enemy partisan activity became problematic immediately, with Marion operating in the low country, Sumter in the midlands, and Pickens in the upstate. The vacillating between conciliation and coercion characterized British leadership throughout the war, and in fact, the most "dead-on" and accurate moment of the whole film occurred when Tom Wilkinson's exasperated and frustrated Cornwallis castigates Tavington for his harsh methods: "His Majesty, like history, judges us not only by the outcome of the war but the manner in which it was fought."[12] Yet, a little later in the film, he unleashes Tavington to do his worst! Indeed, that very scene encapsulates how the British lost the war in the South: an endless cycle of violence between Whig and Tory combined with enemy guerrilla operations (plus the Fabian tactics of one Major General Nathanael Greene).

The settling of old scores was the law of the land. John Postell, a South Carolina militiaman who had been paroled following the surrender of Charleston in May 1780, felt compelled to join Marion's forces after British Legionnaires plundered his home not once but twice. North Carolina militiaman Moses Hall felt the execution of six Loyalist prisoners to be justified after discovering a mortally wounded boy near a recently abandoned British Legion campsite in early 1781. The Ninety-Six District alone supposedly had an estimated 1,400 widows and orphans at the war's end.[13]

Both Whig and Tory were guilty of the most horrendous acts. Yet, responsibility for one's actions and reactions seems to get lost in popular retelling of the conflict. In fact, there seems to be an inherent myth-making undercurrent with the history of the American nation's founding as the misdeeds of some Patriots are conveniently overlooked. As noted aptly by Harvard University History professor Jane Kamensky, to ask whether a myth "is true is to ask the wrong question. It's true to its purposes."[14]

The average American militiaman, even though some current scholars downplay his contribution to the war effort, did play a significant role. More than 164,000 served throughout the conflict,

12   Franklin and Mary Wickwire, *Cornwallis: The American Adventure* (Boston: Houghton Mifflin, 1970); *The Patriot,* DVD.

13   Scotti, *Brutal Virtue,* 1–2 (Hall incident); 74 (Ninety-Six District widows and orphans); 95–96 (Postell incident).

14   Jane Kamensky, "Thankstaking," *Commonplace: The Journal of Early American Life* 1.2 (January 2001), accessed May 13, 2022, www.commonplace.online/article/thankstaking/; see also Scotti, *Brutal Virtue,* 1–11 and 236–237 for the myth-making process and the "usable past."

and as the film portrays, they did admirably at the Battle of the Cowpens in January 1781.[15] And speaking of militia, one of Benjamin Martin's men, Occam (played by the actor Jay Arlen Jones), is African American, which is ironic given that he is representative of a group of people who would not receive their independence for nearly another one hundred years. Black troops are accurately seen in the ranks of both sides in the film. They represented about 7 to 8 percent of American forces, some five thousand total, and all states but South Carolina and Georgia allowed for their enlistment in the Continental Army. Although George Washington did not encourage their participation, he did not turn them away if they appeared in his ranks.[16]

The runaway community at the coast as depicted in the film is something well documented in colonial American history, although it would probably not have been so in the open. Known as "maroons" in the Caribbean and South America, runaways existed as a concomitant problem for the sordid duration of chattel slavery. Major General Anthony Wayne received land from the Georgia State legislature in recognition of his Revolutionary War service, but he had to delay his rice harvest in late 1786 because of locally organized raids on maroon colonies along the Savannah River.[17]

The film's most glaring omission occurs with its treatment of the slavery question. It skirted the hard truth when it portrays freedmen as the labor pool on Martin's farmstead. In reality, it is not very likely that such a backcountry landowner as Martin would have achieved a level of prosperity without the sweat and toil and even blood of enslaved African Americans. Indeed, since the Martin character is a combination of several real historical figures—Marion, Sumter, Pickens, and Morgan—it must be noted that they were all slave owners. The Founding Fathers were indeed flawed human beings, just like the rest of us![18]

French involvement with the American cause appears in the guise of the fictitious Jean Villeneuve (played by the actor Tchéky Karyo), an appropriate reminder that the Thirteen Colonies could not "go at it" alone. The aid of France was essential to the United States being born as an

---

15   Christopher Ward, *The War of the Revolution, 2* volumes (New York: Macmillan, 1952) not only presents an objective assessment of American militia, but it remains by far the best narrative account of the military events surrounding the conflict.

16   South Carolina and Georgia withheld their support for enlisting black soldiers for the obvious reason that whites were in the minority in both states, In fact, by the mid-eighteenth century, Africans accounted for 80 percent of the population in the rice-growing areas of South Carolina. James A. Henretta, et al., *America's History, Volume 1: to 1877,* tenth edition (Boston: Bedford/St. Martin's 2021), 97.

17   Paul David Nelson, *Anthony Wayne: Soldier of the Early Republic* (Bloomington: Indiana University Press, 1985), 206.

18   *The Patriot*, DVD.

independent republic. In fact, from 1775 to 1777, it is estimated that 80 percent of all American gunpowder came from French suppliers.[19]

In conclusion, *The Patriot* stays true to its producers' intent, it is an entertaining drama, suspenseful with great deeds of heroism and villainy. It is full of contradictions, ambiguous at times, and just like real life, it has moments that are neither black nor white. One should be cautioned in viewing it as a good morality play. Nevertheless, if history implicitly begins with questions, then this film proves its worth, as it gets Americans wondering about the true origins of their nation, and that is always a good thing.

---

19   For the surreptitious efforts of French merchants to supply the American colonists before the Franco-American alliance of 1778, see Larrie D. Ferreiro, *Brothers at Arms: American Independence and the Men of France and Spain Who Saved It* (New York: Alfred A. Knopf, 2016), 32–74.

GPS Coordinates

Marker	*
Gravesite/Monument	⚰️
Liberty Trail App Site	🌙
Museum/Visitor Center	🏠
Open Field	🌾
Private Property/Do Not Enter	▦
Ruins	🏚️

Midlands

Site #	Site Name	Latitude	Longitude
1	Rev War Center-Camden 🌙🏠	34.23209°N	80.60515°W
2	Camen-Occupied* 🌙🏠🏚️	34.23326°N	80.60408°W
3	Battle of Hobkirk Hill* 🌙🌾	34.26669° N	80.60089°W
4	Battle of Camden* ⚰️🌾🌙	34.35768° N	80.61029°W
5	Battle of Rugeley's Fort 🌾▦	34.40804°N	80.64398°W
6	Battle of Hanging Rock #1* ⚰️🌙🌾	34.56565°N	80.66175°W
	Battle of Hanging Rock #2* 🌾	34.57151°N	80.68041°W
7	Battle of Waxhaws* ⚰️🌙 (Buford's Massacre)	34.74189°N	80.62587°W
8	Battle of Rocky Mount ⚰️🌾	34.53643°N	80.88478°W
9	Battle of Alexander's Old Fields* 🌾	34.59065°N	80.92006°W
10	Battle of Fishing Creek* 🌾	34.63500°N	80.90417°W
11	Battle of Fishdam Ford* 🌾🏠	34.59444°N	81.41611°W
12	Battle of Huck's Defeat* 🌙🏠 (Brattonsville)	34.86484°N	81.17611°W
13	Battle of Kings Mountain* ⚰️🌙🏠	35.14125°N	81.37718°W

14	Siege of Fort Granby #1	33.97039°N	81.05012°W
15	Battle of Cary's Fort*	34.22100°N	80.63840°W
16	Surrender of Fort Galphin (Fort Dreadnaught)	33.31213°N	81.85563°W

Upstate

Site #	Site Name	Latitude	Longitude
17	Battle of Cowpens*	35.13684°N	81.81837°W
18	Battle of Fort Thicketty	34.98551°N	81.71276°W
19	Battle of Cedar Spring*	34.90931°N	81.87560°W
20	Battle of Wofford's Iron Works*	34.94176°N	81.84532°W
21	Battle of Blackstock's Plantation	34.67917°N	81.81083°W
22	Battle of Musgrove Mill*	34.59331°N	81.85276°W
23	Battle of Great Cane Brake*	34.65576°N	81.31651°W
24	Ring Fight*	34.52980°N	83.29100°W
25	Battle of Lyndley's Fort*	34.45487°N	82.11581°W
26	Hammond's Store Action	34.42570°N	81.87820°W
27	Ninety Six #1*	34.14714°N	82.02341°W
28	Battle of Long Cane*	34.03198°N	82.39416°W

Pee Dee

Site #	Site Name	Latitude	Longitude
29	High Hills of Santee* (Thomas Sumter's Gravesite)	33.98699°N	80.51737°W
30	Battle of Halfway Swamp*	33.65601°N	80.49650°W
31	Siege of Fort Watson*	33.53906°N	80.43662°W
32	Battle of Great Savannah	33.48590°N	80.34482°W
33	Battle of Ox Swamp*	33.42941°N	80.11875°W
34	Battle of Tearcoat Swamp*	33.81166°N	80.14194°W
35	Battle of Blue Savannah*	34.06991°N	79.30709°W
36	Snow's Island*	33.84250°N	79.34111°W
37	Battle of Black Mingo*	33.62234°N	79.43300°W
38	Occupation of Georgetown	33.36715°N	79.28276°W
39	Battle of Kingstree*	33.40359°N	79.50406°W

Lowcountry

Site #	Site Name	Latitude	Longitude
40	Battle of Wambaw Bridge	33.20742°N	79.46878°W
41	Battle of Lenud's Ferry*	33.29441°N	79.68673°W
42	Battle of Biggin Bridge	33.21171°N	79.97880°W
43	Ruins of Biggin Church*	33.21240°N	79.96671°W
44	Battle of Moncks Corner*	33.12187°N	79.59335°W
45	Fairlawn Barony* (Colleton Mansion)		
46	Battle of Wadboo Bridge	33.19577°N	79.95348°W
47	Fort Fairlawn*	33.18639°N	79.97734°W
48	Avenue of Cedars	33.19714°N	79.94195°W
49	Battle of Quinby Bridge*	33.5671°N	79.48435°W
50	Battle of Videau's Bridge	33.02833°N	79.85416°W
51	Battle of Fort Dorchester*	32.94833°N	80.16979°W
52	Breach Inlet Action*	32.77490°N	79.81440°W
	Battle of Fort Sullivan (Fort Moultrie)	32.75911°N	79.85810°W
53	Siege of Charleston*	32.78673°N	79.93633°W
	Fall of Charleston		
54	Hanging Isaac Hayne* (Isaac Hayne's Gravesite)	32.80691°N	80.47918°W
55	Battle of James Island (Dill's Bluff)	32.74712°N	79.944731°W
56	Battle of Stono Ferry	32.74990°N	80.16245°W
57	Jacksonborough—* Provisional Capital of SC	32.76983°N	80.45350°W
58	Battle of Parker's Ferry*	32.85087°N	80.41628°W
59	Battle of Tar Bluff (Combahee Ferry)	32.58494°N	80.57792°W
60	Battle of Port Royal Island*	32.47885°N	80.73715°W
61	Battle of Coosawhatchie Bridge*	32.58843°N	80.92686°W
62	Site of Purrysburg	32.29715°N	81.11942°W
63	Battle of Eutaw Springs*	33.40735°N	80.29858°W
64	Siege of Fort Motte	33.76053°N	80.66978°W

Suggested Sources for Additional Information Online

www.americanbattlefieldtrust.org

www.carolana.com

www.elehistory.com

www.scbattlegroundpreservationtrust.org

www.southerncampaign.org

Suggested Informative Book

"Parker's Guide to the Revolutionary War in South Carolina" by John C. Parker, Jr.

Author Biography

Ms. Humphries was born in Spartanburg, SC, but soon afterwards her family moved to Edgefield County. After graduating from Columbia College with degrees in Special Education and Public Speaking/Drama, she worked at the South Carolina Department of Education and also taught students with special needs. After retiring from the "formal" education system, Aliene continued her passion as an educator by promoting Life-Long Learning.

In 2010, she authored her first book, "The Legacy of a Common Civil War Soldier." This book was based on the letters written by her great-grandfather, Private Thomas Marion Shields during 1861–1865. Aliene authored this book with her maiden name. Same as her paternal great-grandfather.

Presently, Aliene is promoting "The Importance of South Carolina in the American Revolution." Her new book includes 63 sites, plus the new Revolutionary War Visitor Center (in Camden, South Carolina). These sites deserve to be visited, promoted, preserved, and interpreted for us to appreciate. She is hoping to bring more awareness of the important role South Carolina played in helping the 13 colonies become the United States of America, independent from England. The book includes much more information about our great state during this time.

Aliene hopes to communicate the importance of learning more about ourselves and our own family history. Our ancestors (such as Lt. Daniel Gilbert), deserve our respect and being remembered, so we may "connect" and pass information to future generations. She hopes to share this information with those who appreciate "The Importance of South Carolina in the American Revolution."

Aliene is a proud life-long South Carolinian and may be reached via email: Alienehu@yahoo.com